Jane
Seymour

ABOUT THE AUTHOR

DAVID LOADES is Emeritus Professor of the University of Wales and an Honorary Member of the University of Oxford, History Faculty. He is also a Fellow of the Royal Historical Society, Fellow of the Society of Antiquaries and former President of the Ecclesiastical History Society. He is the author of over thirty books. He lives in Burford in Oxfordshire.

PRAISE FOR DAVID LOADES

Henry VIII
'The best place to send anyone seriously wanting to get to grips with alternative understandings of England's most mesmerising monarch ... copious illustrations, imaginatively chosen'
BBC HISTORY MAGAZINE

'A triumph'
THE SPECTATOR

'David Loades' Tudor biographies are both highly enjoyable and instructive, the perfect combination'
ANTONIA FRASER

The Six Wives of Henry VIII
'I warmly recommend this book'
ALISON WEIR

Mary Tudor: A Life
'An excellent and sensitive biography'
THE OBSERVER

Elizabeth I
'Succeeds in depicting her to us as a real woman'
LITERARY REVIEW

'Readable, searching and wise'
NEW STATESMAN

Jane Seymour

Henry VIII's Favourite Wife

DAVID LOADES

AMBERLEY

First published in 2013

This edition first published in 2014

Amberley Publishing
The Hill, Stroud
Gloucestershire, GL5 4EP

www.amberley-books.com

ISBN 978 1 4456 3820 1 (paperback)
ISBN 978 1 4456 1181 5 (ebook)

Typeset in 11pt on 16pt Sabon Lt Std.
Typesetting and Origination by Amberley Publishing
Printed in the UK.

CONTENTS

PREFACE

Jane was Henry VIII's third queen, and was described by him as 'his first true wife', because both his first two marriages had been annulled. She was twenty-seven and had been around the court for some time, so what caused the king to notice her in the early months of 1536 is not known. He may have wanted to annoy his existing queen, Anne Boleyn, in which case he certainly succeeded, provoking an outburst which contributed to her downfall. By all accounts Jane was no beauty, and had no intellectual interests, but she was reasonably accomplished in the 'domestic arts', such as needlework. She was also a virgin, and came of a good breeding stock; her father, Sir John Seymour, having sired several sons before she was born. All these factors would have commended her to Henry. Above all she was good-natured and docile, characteristics which appealed to a king on the rebound from Anne's feisty and aggressive personality. When he tested her with a present, and probably a proposition in February 1536, she returned his letter unopened, but with a submissive message professing her virtue. This seems to have stimulated Henry's enthusiasm, and within days of Anne's execution they were betrothed. Beyond interceding for her friend, the Lady Mary, Jane played little part in the tangled politics of late 1536 and early 1537, but it is necessary to know how the king was occupied while Jane presided at his court, attracting the favourable notice of all and sundry. Her father died in December and for that and a number of other reasons her Coronation was postponed, and then in February 1537 she became pregnant, causing a further postponement. She was, apparently, warned off political involvement and told to concentrate on the business of producing an heir. This she successfully did in October, and Henry was immensely gratified at this seal of divine approval upon all his enterprises. Edward's birth, however, was quickly followed by the death of his mother, and the king's joy turned to grief. With her elaborate interment at Windsor in November, Jane's story really comes to an end, but she left a number of legacies behind her, which carried her presence forward into the years ahead. Henry had to be persuaded to take a new wife, and that search dominated his foreign policy for the next two and a half years. There was also a growing prince to be nurtured and cared for. His education was of the utmost importance, and was probably not at all what Jane, with her conservative piety, would have wanted. The Act of Six Articles would have been more to her taste! She also left behind at the court two brothers, Edward and Thomas, who had made their careers partly through her influence. Edward became Viscount Beauchamp and Earl of Hertford because of his relationship with the queen, and Thomas made a promising start in the Privy Chamber. Both were soldiers, and Edward, particularly, was a statesman of importance in the last years of Henry's reign. After the king's death, he became Duke of Somerset and Lord Protector during Edward's minority, but fell out seriously with his brother, who was executed in March 1549. Following his own overthrow in October 1549 he appeared to be reconciled to his supplanter, John Dudley, then the Earl of Warwick, and later the Duke of Northumberland, but they subsequently quarrelled and he was himself dispatched on a charge of felony in January 1552.

The duke's execution brought to an end the careers of those who had been dependent upon Jane, and the young king's premature death the following July brought the end of her direct bloodline. Politically, the aftermath of her life was more important than when she was queen, but she had a profound effect upon Henry, and that in itself makes her worth a study. We know so little about her early life that this inevitably concentrates upon her year-and-a-bit as queen, and upon the legacy which she left behind. Many years of reading and research lie behind this work, and acknowledgements too numerous to mention, but I would like to thank Jonathan Reeve of Amberley Publishing for suggesting that I undertake it, and my wife Judith for her constant and knowledgeable support.

David Loades,
Burford, October 2012.

A NOTE ON TITLES

Sir Thomas Boleyn, father of Anne, Mary and George, became Viscount Rochford in 1525, and Earl of Wiltshire and Ormond in 1529.

George Boleyn became Viscount Rochford in 1529.

Anne Boleyn became Marquis of Pembroke in 1532.

Edward Seymour became Viscount Beauchamp in 1536, Earl of Hertford in 1537 and Duke of Somerset in 1547.

Thomas Seymour became Lord Seymour of Sudeley in 1547.

John Dudley became Viscount Lisle in 1542, Earl of Warwick in 1547 and Duke of Northumberland in 1551.

William Parr became Lord Parr in 1539, Earl of Essex in 1543, and Marquis of Northampton in 1547. Forfeited in 1554, he was restored in 1559.

Thomas Wriothesley became Lord Wriothesley in 1544, and Earl of Southampton in 1547.

Henry Fitzroy became Earl of Nottingham, and Duke of Richmond and Somerset in 1525.

Thomas Howard became Earl of Surrey in 1514, and Duke of Norfolk in 1524. Forfeited in 1546, he was restored in 1553.

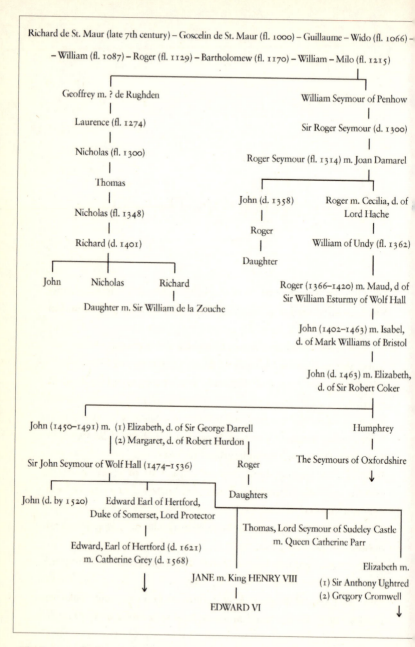

Richard de St. Maur (late 7th century) – Goscelin de St. Maur (fl. 1000) – Guillaume – Wido (fl. 1066) –

– William (fl. 1087) – Roger (fl. 1129) – Bartholomew (fl. 1170) – William – Milo (fl. 1215)

Geoffrey m. ? de Rughden

Laurence (fl. 1274)

Nicholas (fl. 1300)

Thomas

Nicholas (fl. 1348)

Richard (d. 1401)

John   Nicholas   Richard

Daughter m. Sir William de la Zouche

William Seymour of Penhow

Sir Roger Seymour (d. 1300)

Roger Seymour (fl. 1314) m. Joan Damarel

John (d. 1358)

Roger

Daughter

Roger m. Cecilia, d. of Lord Hache

William of Undy (fl. 1362)

Roger (1366–1420) m. Maud, d of Sir William Esturmy of Wolf Hall

John (1402–1463) m. Isabel, d. of Mark Williams of Bristol

John (d. 1463) m. Elizabeth, d. of Sir Robert Coker

John (1450–1491) m. (1) Elizabeth, d. of Sir George Darrell
(2) Margaret, d. of Robert Hurdon

Sir John Seymour of Wolf Hall (1474–1536)

Humphrey

The Seymours of Oxfordshire ↓

John (d. by 1520)   Edward Earl of Hertford, Duke of Somerset, Lord Protector

Roger

Daughters

Edward, Earl of Hertford (d. 1621) m. Catherine Grey (d. 1568)

Thomas, Lord Seymour of Sudeley Castle m. Queen Catherine Parr

Elizabeth m.
(1) Sir Anthony Ughtred
(2) Gregory Cromwell ↓

↓

JANE m. King HENRY VIII

EDWARD VI

1. The Seymour family genealogical table.

I

INTRODUCTION:
THE FAMILY AT WOLF HALL

Jane was very conscious of her lineage. When, at a fairly crucial point in her prenuptial relations with Henry VIII, she described herself as coming of an ancient and honourable family, she was not exaggerating.[1] With the aid of some imaginative speculation the Seymours traced their origins back to the village of Saint-Maur-sur-Loir, and to the supposed head of that village, one Richard de St. Maur, who is thought to have lived in the late seventh century. A Guy de St. Maur, who may have been his son, performed homage and fealty to the Abbey of Villers for the same lands in 701. Thereafter the story runs through unknown generations, via a certain Ludo de St. Maur, who is alleged to have been alive in 919, to slightly firmer ground with Goscelin de St. Maur, who is mentioned in a charter of Foulque Martel, Comte d'Anjou dated to the year 1000. He was styled 'Castri Sanctae Maurae dei gratia hereditario possessor et dominus' (of the castle of St Maur by the grace of God hereditary owner and lord) and Pope Gregory VII wrote him a letter.[2] Goscelin married in about 1009, and had four sons, the eldest of whom seems, rather unusually, to have been a priest. It was through the second son, Guillaume, that the connection with England arose, because Guillaume's son, Wido, appears to have accompanied the Conqueror in 1066. This cannot be firmly established because of the incompleteness of the surviving lists, but Wido de St. Maur received a barony which extended into Somerset, Wiltshire and Gloucestershire, and that argues some significant service. He seems to have died at some point before 1087, because at the time of the Domesday Survey the barony was held by his son, known as William Fitz-Wido.[3] Nothing much is known of William or his circumstances, but he seems to have had a son, Roger, who was born at some point before 1100 and appears as a witness to a charter of Richard de Cormeil to the Priory of Monmouth, which can be dated with some certainty to 1129. Roger had some association with the county of Monmouth, and may already have settled at Penhow, which the family certainly owned not many years later. It may be that Roger had been given some responsibility in the Marches of Wales, although this cannot be proved. A Bartholomew de Sancto Mauro, who was almost certainly his son, witnessed a charter of William, Earl of Gloucester to Keynsham Abbey in about 1170, and his son, another William, was one of the king's esquires in 1175.[4] In 1215 we find a Milo de St. Maur among the barons who forced King John to sign the Magna Carta, and since he is described as a descendant of Roger, he was presumably William's son, although nothing very much is known about his career beyond the fact that he is named in the Fine Roll of King John.

Milo left two sons, Geoffrey and William, and from them two branches of the St. Maur (or Seymour) family descended. The first, which was based at Kingston Seymour in Somerset, ran through five generations and ended with a daughter, Alice, who married Sir William Zouche in the early fifteenth century.[5] The second family, descended from William, was based at Penhow. For some reason the two families denied any connection with each other, and adopted quite distinct coats of arms. It may be that Milo married twice, or even that William was illegitimate, although the fact that he inherited Penhow makes the latter unlikely. It was from this family that Queen Jane was descended. Geoffrey married a daughter of William de Rughdon and left a son, Laurence, who in 1274 was granted by Edward I a market to be held at his manor of Rode in Somerset and an annual fair to be held on the morrow of St Margaret the Virgin (21 July). He acknowledged the service of half a knight's fee for his lands in Wiltshire in 1282, and shortly after was involved in the king's campaigns in Wales.[6] He died in about 1297 and was succeeded by his son Nicholas, who went abroad in the Crown's service in that same year. Nicholas was also summoned for military service against the Scots in 1298 and 1300. In 1306 he was in the retinue of Henry of Lancaster, and in 1313 was pardoned for having been involved in the death of Piers Gaveston, King Edward II's favourite. At that same time he was summoned to parliament as a representative of Gloucestershire, and served again against the Scots on a number of occasions over the next few years. In 1316 he was certified as the lord of a number of manors in Gloucester, Herefordshire, Wiltshire and Somerset. He died in 1317, leaving his son Thomas under-age, and the latter's wardship was granted to Hugh Despenser the elder in settlement of debts owed to him by the Crown.[7] Thomas did not long survive his minority, but lived long enough to marry and to father an heir, Nicholas, who was old enough in 1348 to serve in the retinue of Maurice de Berkeley in France, a feat which he repeated with Thomas de Holland in 1360. He was also a member of parliament from 1352 to 1361, in which year he died, leaving his extensive estates to his second son, Richard. Richard also served in France in 1387 in the retinue of his namesake, the Earl of Arundel, and was summoned to parliament from 1381 to 1401, in which year he died. He left three sons, but of these the eldest, Richard, died in 1408, leaving only an infant daughter, as we have seen. In due course she married Sir William Zouche of Totnes in Devon who performed fealty and had livery of her lands. John and Nicholas died without issue.

Meanwhile Milo's second son, William, known as Sir William de St. Maur, knight of Penhow, had dug himself into the Welsh Marches. In 1235–6, with the connivance of William Marshall, Earl of Pembroke, he wrested the manor of Undy from Morgan ap Howell, a Welshman and Lord of Caerleon, in the course of a border campaign.[8] Penhow remained his principal residence, however, and he rebuilt the castle, creating a large park for the benefit of his hunting. He also erected a church in the vicinity, which he dedicated to St Maur, who was clearly the patron saint of the family. Sir William's signature appears as witness on several charters of Gilbert and Walter Marshall, kinsmen of the Earl of Pembroke, one of which is dated 1245, and he married Earl William's third daughter, but nothing else in known about his career. He had died by 1269, when his son Sir Roger de St. Maur is mentioned a Lord of the Manor of Undy. Nothing is known of this Sir Roger, other than the fact that he married and died at some point before 1300, when he had been succeeded by his son, also Roger. There is no mention of a minority, so this Roger must have been born before 1280, which would date his father's marriage to a few years previous to that. Of this Roger nothing much is known except that he was alive in 1314 and that he married Joan, the daughter of one Damarel of Devonshire. The date of his death is not known, but he left two sons by Joan, John and Roger. John died in about 1358, leaving a son Roger, who had been born in about 1340. This Roger lived long enough to marry and father a child – a daughter whose name is not known, but who subsequently married one of the Bowlays of Monmouthshire, and conveyed her inheritance of Penhow into that family.[9] Meanwhile John's younger brother, confusingly also called Roger, became Lord of the Manor of Undy in succession to his father, but appears not to have spent much time there, preferring to reside at Evinswinden (or Swindon) in Wiltshire. He married Cecilia, daughter of John de Beauchamp, Baron of Hache in Somerset, who was descended from William

Marshall, Earl of Pembroke, whose links with the family earlier we have noticed. Cecilia was co-heiress of John, and her marriage to Roger Seymour (as we may now call him) greatly enhanced both the importance and the wealth of the Seymour family. John died in 1363 and his lands were divided between his two daughters.[10] Cecilia outlived Roger by a number of years, so he never enjoyed that inheritance. She died in 1393, having also outlived her eldest son, William, who died in 1390. About this William again not very much is known, apart from the fact that he resided mainly at Undy, and is mentioned in 1362 as attending the Prince of Wales in the government of Gascony, which presumably means that he was born not later than about 1340. He married Margaret, the daughter of Simon de Brockburn, and their son – yet another Roger – was born in 1366, inheriting his grandmother's extensive lands on her death. A little before 1400 he married Maud, the daughter and co-heir of Sir William Esturmy, knight, of Wolf Hall, Wiltshire, and it was through her inheritance that Wolf Hall came into the possession of the Seymour family.[11] The Esturmys had also been hereditary Wardens of Savernake Forest since the days of Henry III, and the bearers of the symbolic hunting horn which signified that status. This office, too, came to Roger Seymour in the right of his wife, and he presumably also inherited the patronage of the hospital of the Holy Trinity at Easton, near Marlborough, which the Esturmys had founded many years earlier. Roger died in 1420, and was succeeded in his numerous properties by his son John, who had been born in 1402. There is no reference to any wardship, so presumably he was deemed to be of full age. He was also the heir of his cousin, Sir Peter de la Mere, and was thus a man of very considerable substance.

In 1430, at the age of twenty-eight, he was chosen as Sheriff of Hampshire, and in the following year served Wiltshire in the same capacity.[12] As far as we know he was the first member of the family to be selected for this office, which may reflect a change in royal policy during the minority of King Henry VI, or (more likely) his greatly enhanced wealth, which made a leading role in the affairs of the counties more or less inevitable. He was knighted in 1432, an honour which seems to have owed less to his service in the field than to his administrative ability. In a return dated 1434 his name appears first, after that of William Westbury, who was royal justice and a member of the council. In the same year he was Sheriff of Gloucester and Somerset, an indication of the extent of his estates, because it was normal to select a leading landowner of the county for this onerous but powerful responsibility. In 1437 he was selected again for Hampshire, but served only once more (for Wiltshire in 1450) during the fraught years of Henry's personal government.[13] In 1440 he sat for Wiltshire in the parliament which was held at Reading, and in 1454 was a member of the commission of array issued to the county with a view to raising forces against the Duke of York. Thereafter he served regularly on commissions: of the Peace from 1453 to 1458; to investigate piracy in April 1457; 'for beacons' in September of the same year; and of array in 1457, 1458 and 1459 as the civil war escalated. More significantly in 1458 he was granted a pardon because, as Sheriff of Wiltshire again in that year, he had allowed a felon to escape, and in September 1459 was commissioned to put down insurrections in the county.[14] The impression given is that of a loyal servant of the House of Lancaster, but it should probably be that of a loyal servant of the king *in situ*, because there is no sign of his favour diminishing between the Yorkist victory in 1461 and his death in 1463. If he ever raised his own men to participate in the wars there is no record of it, and he seems to have been nearly as neutral as a man of his substance could be.

In 1424, John married Isabel, the daughter of Mark Williams of Bristol, a match which may well have enhanced his connections with the mercantile elite but did nothing for his wealth in other ways. She held several properties in Bristol but, owing to the fact that he predeceased her, none of them ever came to him. Nor did their son (also John) inherit, because he died a couple of months before his father in 1463. This John had, in around 1448, married Elizabeth, the daughter of Sir Robert Coker of Laurence Lydiard, Somerset, and when he died he left two sons, John and Humphrey, both under-age. The wardship seems to have been granted to their mother, who lived until 1472, by which time both boys were able to inherit. Humphrey, the younger brother, settled at Swindon and married the daughter and co-heir of Thomas Winslow of Burton in Oxfordshire. It was from him that the Seymours of Oxfordshire and Gloucestershire descended, but they are not part of this story.[15] The elder brother John, who was born around 1450, received Wolf Hall, but unlike his father seems to have served on no county commissions until after 1480, perhaps because of his youth and inexperience However, like his father and grandfather, he then served the Crown impartially and seems not to have taken sides in the quarrels that arose in 1483. He was a subsidy commissioner for Wiltshire in 1483, and a commissioner of array for the county in 1484, at which point Richard III was getting worried about potential challenges to his power. In June 1485 he was granted a survey (known as an exemplification) of the bounds of Savernake Forest, and in the same month was placed on a commission to deal with riots in the county of Wiltshire.[16] Nevertheless in February 1486 the new king Henry VII tidied up a fifteen-year-old omission in the legitimacy of his position by granting John livery and right of entry to his grandfather's lands, which should have been done when he achieved his majority, but appears to have been overlooked.[17] If Henry had entertained any doubts about the loyalty of John Seymour, it would have been easy to withhold such recognition, but he seems to have made the transition to the new regime without a stain upon his honour or credibility. He married twice, and by his first wife Elizabeth, the daughter of Sir George Darrell of Littlecote, Wiltshire he had four sons and four daughters; by his second wife Margaret, daughter of Robert Hardon, he had one son, Roger. Roger left only daughters as his co-heirs and they play no part in the story, but the four sons of his first marriage all grew up and had careers of their own. John, the eldest, was the father of Queen Jane, while George was Sheriff of Wilshire in 1499, and William was made a Knight of the Bath at the marriage of Prince Arthur with Catherine of Aragon in November 1501.[18] Robert was later a Gentleman Usher of the Chamber. The elder John died in 1491, leaving his heir of the same name, who had been born in around 1474, well short of his majority. An inquisition post-mortem was held on 30 May 1492 in order to establish what lands in Somerset John Seymour had held at the time of his death, and the identity of his heir. This suggests a degree of uncertainty about those lands, because no similar inquisition was held for Wiltshire, where the inheritance was apparently unchallenged. On 26 December 1493 the wardship and marriage of John junior was granted to Sir Henry Wentworth, and it may well have been as a result that John married Margery, Sir Henry's daughter, at some time before 1498.[19] He served the king in arms at the Battle of Blackheath in 1497, and attracted sufficient favourable attention to receive the honour of knighthood on the field. He was Sheriff of Wiltshire in 1497–8, and was named to the Commission of the Peace for that county from 1499 until his death in 1536.

Sir John's career thereafter was focussed mainly on Wiltshire and its neighbouring counties, his presence at court being low-key. He was steward of the Duke of Buckingham's lands in the county by 1503 and served as sheriff again in 1507–8 and in 1525–6. He was also Sheriff of Somerset and Dorset in 1515–6 and again in 1526–7. A subsidy commissioner for Wiltshire in 1512, 1514 and 1525, he served for both the county and the town of Salisbury in 1524, and was a member of just about every commission issued for the three counties throughout the reign, until the time of his death.[20] He seems to have been regularly present at court, but this was little remarked on, possibly because he was not one of the king's companions. He had no taste for jousting, and seems not to have participated in the royal revels.[21] He was Knight of the Body at the very beginning of Henry VIII's reign, but this conferred no intimacy, and was probably no more than a recognition of his local importance. Henry was keen to build bridges to the gentry communities of the counties, and Sir John Seymour seems to have been a good example of how that connection worked. Towards the end of his life, in 1532, he was created a Groom of the Privy Chamber, but this again seems to have been a recognition of his status rather than of any close relationship with the king. He attended Henry VII's funeral, for which he received a livery grant, and he and Margery both appeared in the pardon roll of the new king, presumably to cover any possible comeback from his year as sheriff. More significantly, he bore a banner at the funeral of the short-lived Prince Henry in February 1511. That was a mark of favour, and may have been connected with Sir John's developing role as a military servant of the Crown.[22] In 1512 we find him (rather unexpectedly) serving alongside Sir Charles Brandon on the *Dragon of Greenwich*, one of the ships taken up for naval service in the following year, although whether he actually sailed on her is not known. Shortly after he was listed as leading 100 men for the abortive Brittany campaign of May 1513, and that may explain his possible presence on board, because the naval campaign was intended to be the preparation for an invasion.[23] However it is likely that his role in that expedition was aborted and that he and his 100 men were diverted to the army royal which the king led into Picardy in June, because he certainly served in that campaign, being present at the siege of Thèrouanne, and also at the Battle of the Spurs. It was for his valour in the latter engagement that he was awarded the status of Knight Banneret, although his part again evaded the attentions of the chroniclers. In 1523 he served under the Duke of Suffolk on his winter campaign in northern France, and his part in that expedition is similarly obscure. By that time he appears to have been a part of the military furniture, and at the age of forty-seven or forty-eight may well have been a member of the staff rather than an active field commander.[24]

Sir John Seymour had been granted the constableship of Bristol Castle in August 1509, and that grant was renewed in survivorship with his son Edward in July 1517. Edward was about seventeen at that time, so his father was clearly looking ahead! Neither Edward nor Margery accompanied John on his next assignment at court, however. He went with the king to the Field of Cloth of Gold in 1520, for which he was allowed eleven servants, but there is no mention of Margery featuring among the queen's attendants.[25] He also took part in some obscure capacity in the meetings with Charles V which both preceded and followed Henry's encounter with Francis I. On the second occasion he was one of those designated to accompany the Emperor, and this led many years later to Eustace Chapuys describing him as having been once in Charles's service. This may have been technically true if Charles paid the expenses of his escort.[26] In 1529 John served on the commission appointed to assess the possessions of Cardinal Wolsey in Wiltshire following the latter's fall from grace, and in 1532 accompanied the king and the Marquis of Pembroke to their meeting with Francis I at Calais, as a representative, it would seem, of the county of Wiltshire. There are various other references to Sir John in the records. In 1518, for example, he is described as a 'gentleman of the palace' in the arrangements for the French embassy of that year; he received a number of wardships and became embroiled in a legal dispute with the Bishop of Salisbury over the alleged theft of two oxen.[27] He may have sat in parliament in the early part of Henry VIII's reign, the records of which are missing. That would certainly have been consistent with his status, but the only occasion upon which it can be demonstrated was in 1529, when he sat for the borough of Heytesbury, having lost the county nomination to Sir Edward

Darrell and Sir Edward Baynton. If he did anything of note during the sessions which followed, it has escaped the record.[28] In spite of occasional bouts of litigation he seems to have been an amiable man, well liked in his local community, and his quarrel with Sir William Essex is an obscure episode, knowledge of which depends upon a single appeal made to Thomas Cromwell in 1532.

Sir John married, as we have seen, in about 1498, the date being deducible from the birth of his second son, Edward in 1500. His first-born, named for his father, was probably born in 1499, and had died unmarried by 1520. Whether he survived his minority or not is unclear, but since he does not feature in any record, the chances are that he did not.[29] Edward may have been introduced to the court as a child, and was about fourteen when he was placed as a page of honour in the retinue which Mary Rose, the king's sister, took with her when she married Louis XII of France in the autumn of 1514. However, he cannot have stayed long in France, as the king dismissed most of his wife's English attendants within days of their marriage, an episode which caused a certain *froideur* in their relationship.[30] On his return he is alleged to have spent some time at the universities of both Oxford and Cambridge, but if so he left no mark in the records and certainly did not take a degree. That, however, would have been normal for a young gentleman at that time, who customarily spent a few months or years giving themselves a gloss which might come in useful in dealing with a court where education was increasingly valued. Sir John may not have had much taste for court life himself, but he seems to have been determined that his son would make a mark there. In July 1525, when the king was creating a household for his bastard son, newly created Duke of Richmond, he named Sir Edward Seymour as Master of the Horse, which was a senior and responsible position, carrying a fee of £60 a year.[31] Edward had earned his knighthood when he had accompanied his father on the Duke of Suffolk's campaign in 1523, an adventure in which he seems to have distinguished himself, receiving his recognition on the field of battle. In 1524 he had become an esquire of the king's household, and in February 1525 had joined his father on the Commission of the Peace for Wiltshire. He accompanied Cardinal Wolsey on his trip to France in 1527 in search of a solution to the king's 'Great Matter' – his desire to secure an annulment of his first marriage, which the Pope was refusing. However he was not in any sense in Wolsey's service. 1527 was a crucial year in Henry's matrimonial affairs, because that was the year in which he proposed marriage to Anne Boleyn, and thereby committed himself to the ending of his existing relationship.[32] For the next two years, as Wolsey struggled with this intractable problem, Anne maintained towards him an attitude of scrupulous amiability, seeing him, and persuading the king, that he was the only man capable of resolving it. However, when the Legatine Court, which Clement VII had commissioned to hear the case, was adjourned in the summer of 1529, with no resolution in sight, her attitude changed. Wolsey's Roman connections had proved useless, and Anne became convinced that only a unilateral declaration of independence would provide an answer. The cardinal thus became an obstacle rather than an asset, and she used her unique influence with the king to bring about his downfall in the autumn of 1529.[33] In these events the Seymours played no recognised part. Sir John was not a supporter of the Boleyns – if anything his sympathies were on the other side – but he was only a peripheral member of the court, and his opinions did not much matter; while Sir Edward, who was undoubtedly a courtier, was not close to the centres of power. His favour seems to have been unaffected by these momentous events. In March 1529 he was granted the stewardship of the manors of Hengstage and Charleton in Somerset, which had been held by Sir William Compton, and in September 1530 he received an annuity of 50 marks (£33) a year as an Esquire of the Body, which presumably indicates the fact that he was expected to be in regular attendance.[34]

His uncle Robert, Sir John's younger brother, also received some marks of favour, and by 1529 had been appointed a Gentleman Usher of the Chamber, which would have involved attendance for a part of each year on a kind of shift system, and did not carry any fees except when on duty. The same Robert was granted the stewardship of the manors of Amesbury and Winterbourne in July 1526 and the shrievalty of distant Anglesey in January 1527. This last office was in the gift of the Crown as a part of the Principality of Wales, and would have been discharged by deputy. There is no indication that Robert Seymour went to live in North Wales.[35] Very little is known about him, but he was also granted the Wardenship of Melchet Forest in Wiltshire in 1529, which was in the hands of the king because of the minority of Sir William Compton's son Peter. These promotions may have been due to Wolsey's favour, and would not have been made without his approval, but we know nothing of the relationship which Robert (or any of the Seymours) had with the cardinal. The one thing that is certain is that recognition of the service of the family goes back well before any interest which the king showed in their sister Jane.

Jane was Sir John's eldest daughter, although something like his fourth or fifth child, and had been born, probably at Wolf Hall, in 1508 or 1509. His ability to father sons was something of a joke between him and the king before the subject became too bitter for jest, and the appearance of a daughter at this point may well have been something of a relief to him, as well as to Margery. Nothing is known of her childhood or upbringing, which presumably took place at home under the watchful eye of her mother. It was quite normal in those days to put children out at the age of about seven or eight, to be brought up in a neighbouring household, but there is no indication of that happening to Jane, or to any of her siblings.[36] Like them she would have been taught first at home, probably by a chaplain of her father's. Later in life she was certainly literate, but appears to have had no knowledge of Latin, that gateway to the world of learning which only the most advanced educationalists thought suitable for girls. Goodness knows what loose morals they might have picked up if they had got hold of a copy of the Roman poet Ovid! Her reading would have been strictly monitored to make sure that no 'light and lascivious' tales came to her attention, because a maiden's chastity was her most prized possession. This seems to have been a lesson which Jane learned very thoroughly, along with the needlework and household management which would have formed the rest of her domestic curriculum. An early marriage into a suitable gentle family would have been her expected fate, and the reasons why that did not happen are obscure. Perhaps in the 1520s Sir John' resources were stretched and he could not find a sufficient dowry to satisfy the families of potential suitors. There is an indication of that in 1523, when he asked the king for a remission of his loan payment; he undertook to pay in full, but requested more time to find the money.[37] As he was a subsidy commissioner shortly afterwards, this admission was an embarrassment of some significance, but we cannot be sure that it affected Jane's prospects. Rather surprisingly she seems to have remained at home, unwed and unbidden for, until 1529 when Sir John (or possibly Sir Edward) found a place for her in the household of the queen. It may well be that she had been introduced to the court before that date, and been in the service of some senior lady, but there is no trace of her in the records. She was, according to later accounts, no great beauty, but remarkable for the sweetness of her disposition, and it may well have been that characteristic which enabled her to transfer to the service of Queen Anne when Catherine's household was reduced in the summer of 1533.[38] There is no suggestion that at that stage the king had any particular interest in her, his attention being focussed entirely upon Anne until the time when she was declared to be pregnant in January 1533.

Meanwhile Jane's relations continued to enjoy the royal favour in various fairly modest ways. Both Edward and John borrowed money of the king in 1532, apparently through the mediation of

Thomas Cromwell. The former had £1,000 and the latter £2,000, which they undertook to repay in regular instalments. Sir Edward's loan may well have been to enable him to purchase the manor of Eastham in Somerset and other lands from Edward, Lord Bray, but the reason for Sir John's indebtedness is not known.[39] As early as 1531 John was sending Cromwell a 'tagg of his own killing' as an inducement to favour him in his quarrel with Sir William Essex, which we have already noted.[40] In February 1532 Sir Edward also entered into a complex transaction with Lord Lisle for the purchase of the reversion of Cheddar Norton and other lands in Somerset, but apparently had difficulty in obtaining recognition of his title with the result that a dispute arose between them which took some three years to resolve and resulted in considerable bitterness. In July 1533 Edward Windsor wrote to Lord Lisle to say that his counsel had held several meetings with Edward 'about the bargain of the lands which he bought of your Lordship, but Master Denzil and Master Morgan (Edward's counsel), say that you have not kept covenant with him in entering your lands again, and that he was bound to make your Lordship a lease for the term of your life of £140'. Edward was insisting upon having possession, and no agreement had been reached.[41] An action for debt was being taken out against Lisle, presumably for non-payment of the £140. Lisle's officers, particularly his auditor John Smith, tried to bring pressure to bear upon Seymour to abandon this suit, but to no effect. In November of the same year Lisle lodged a complaint against Sir Edward on the grounds that he had got him to sign an indenture to his own prejudice. Some kind of fraud seems to have been implied, although that was not stated. The lands concerned were a part of those which Lisle had received from his first wife – consequently he had only a life interest in them – and they seem to have been subject to an arrangement, known as an enfeoffment to use, in the interest of James Basset, Honor Lisle's son by her first marriage. This no doubt complicated the question of sale, and made the resulting legal tangle one of particular density.[42] An arbitration was eventually agreed in February 1534, but that was by no means the end of the matter.

Meanwhile Sir Edward had consolidated his favour at court by exchanging New Year gifts with the king in 1532 and 1533. These exchanges were normal for members of the nobility, but below that level were indicative of membership of the inner ring of courtiers, and by no means guaranteed to one who was only an Esquire of the Body. Whatever Lord Lisle may have thought, it seems that Edward was closer to Cromwell than he was, which may explain why he pursued his quarrel with such tenacity. Sooner or later the secretary was bound to intervene on his side. He also married. At some point before 1518 he had married Catherine, the daughter and co-heir of Sir William Fillol, who had lands in Dorset and in Essex. They had two sons, John and Edward, but it was not a happy union. At some point after 1530 Sir Edward repudiated her, alleging misconduct, and their sons had no share in his subsequent titles.[43] They had honourable but low-key careers. John was MP for Wootton Bassett in Wiltshire in 1547, and died comparatively young in 1552, while Edward, who lived until 1593, was knighted at the Battle of Pinkie during the invasion of Scotland in 1547 – presumably by his father, who commanded that expedition – but secured no other mark of recognition. There was no suggestion that they were illegitimate, and they were provided for out of their mother's inheritance. When she died in 1535 the responsibility for their upbringing must have reverted to Sir Edward Seymour, because no wardship was declared. The younger, who had been born in 1529, was certainly under-age, and both may have been, but when Edward remarried on 9 March 1535, his second wife Anne Stanhope wanted nothing to do with them, and they must have been brought up at some distance from the court by servants who were answerable to Edward, but they had no share in his future, which was reserved to his children with Anne. Jane, for all her amiable disposition, never seems to have shown the slightest interest in her nephews.

She, meanwhile, had caught the royal eye. Eustace Chapuys, the Imperial ambassador, was an implacable foe of Anne Boleyn and all that she stood for. He was consequently on the lookout for Henry's 'amours', which might be useful in undermining her position.[44] In October 1534 he reported that a certain young lady was increasingly in credit with the king, and although he did not name her, this lady was almost certainly Jane.[45] She, however, had no incentive to fall out with Anne, whose servant she was. Although they may well have been sympathetic to Catherine, the Seymours seem to have been comfortable enough with the Boleyn ascendancy. Or at least, if they were not, the king had not noticed. Edward had served as a carver at Anne's Coronation, an honour which he could have evaded if he had been so minded, and Jane, of course, was in attendance on her mistress. Thomas, Sir Edward's younger brother, was probably also present as a junior member of the household, and the elderly Sir John's absence would not have been remarked upon. However, like all passionate relationships, Henry's marriage had its ups and downs, and in the summer of 1534 Anne had miscarried of her second child. Her first, Elizabeth, had been a disappointment, but this second misfortune seems to have awakened the king's old demons. Suppose, after all, he had been mistaken in Anne, and she was not to be their mother of his heir?[46] His eye began to stray, and it was at this point that Jane seems to have come 'in credit' with Henry. Anne reacted badly, and although on this occasion the relationship was patched up, and the queen returned to favour, a warning had been given. Anne does not seem to have known the identity of her temporary rival, which was just as well, but the seeds of doubt had been sown. Edward, who does not seem to have missed much that was going on and was in touch with Chapuys, must have realised that his sister was in a very promising, if vulnerable, situation. What Sir John thought, we do not know. He does not feature at all in the records for 1534, even as a Commissioner of the Peace, and it may well be that his health was failing, but he was probably blessing that fortune which had dispatched Jane to court as a virgin and had *mirabile dictu*, kept her in that condition, despite the temptations with which she must have been beset.

2

JANE & ANNE

How Jane came to enter Queen Catherine's service in 1529 is something of a mystery. She was about twenty years old, and is unlikely to have been a newcomer to the court. The natural assumption is that she must have been attendant upon some peeress who would have brought her to the royal attention, but there is no record of who that might have been. Bearing in mind the difficulties which Honor, Lady Lisle, had a few years later in securing a similar preferment for the daughter of her first marriage, Anne Basset, whoever Jane's original patron may have been, she (or he) was obviously a person of great influence.[1] The only member of her kindred who was regularly at court in these years was her brother, Sir Edward, and although he was in good standing with the king, there is no reason to suppose that he would have had the ability to place his sister in such exalted company.[2] Perhaps he was able to intercede with one of the female patronage brokers, such as the Countess of Sussex, who was able to introduce this unknown damsel to the royal circle. The records are silent on the subject, which is not surprising; after all we know very little of the means by which Anne Boleyn had been appointed about seven years before, except that in her case the obvious agent was her father, who was not only a diplomat in high favour but was also the father of Mary Boleyn, the current royal mistress. His influence is not far to seek, although no one commented upon it at the time. Jane must also have been acceptable to Catherine herself, because no one could be placed in her service without her consent. The queen was not looking for beauty, or great intelligence. She did not expect to have intellectual discussions with her attendants; but she was looking for piety, and for an ability to fit in to the demanding schedules of daily attendance. She was also probably looking for domestic skills such as needlework, and for an ability to divert the pressing attentions of male courtiers with too little to do, through the game of courtly love or otherwise.[3] Dalliance was not one of the skills which she had learned at Wolf Hall, and unlike Anne at a similar stage, she had not attracted the serious attentions of any eligible male. Marriage, which was always the prime objective of the unattached members of the queen's Privy Chamber, must have seemed a long way off for Jane. Nor was this a matter in which the queen was disposed (or perhaps able) to be very helpful. Mistress Seymour presumably took part in a modest way in the revels of these years, but as relations between the king and queen became increasingly strained, these were neither as frequent nor as splendid as in times past, and not even Edward Hall noticed her participation. As far as Catherine was concerned, she was a part of the furniture, and as long as she went to mass and did not draw attention to herself, that situation seemed likely to continue.

It did not do so because Catherine's own position collapsed in the early part of 1533. She had reacted with outrage to the king's attempts to repudiate their marriage, which went back to the summer of 1527, and had taken refuge in 1529 in a direct appeal to the Pope.[4] She had also sought the aid of her nephew, the Emperor Charles V, so that if Henry was going to have his way, it would have to be by the rejection of all authorities outside the realm. She knew by 1530 the identity of her supplanter in the royal affections, but was powerless to do anything about it, so Anne Boleyn remained nominally one of her ladies until she was created

Marquis of Pembroke in September 1532. By that time Henry had steeled himself for the inevitable, and Anne became complaisant. Probably during a trip to Calais in October, they slept together and she became pregnant. Since the ultimate driving force behind this whole 'Great Matter' was the king's urgent need for a son and heir, it was essential that the child that Anne was carrying should be born legitimate, and Henry forced his newly appointed Archbishop of Canterbury, Thomas Cranmer, to declare his marriage to Catherine null and void in April 1533.[5] The king had already secretly married Anne, and on 1 June she was solemnly crowned as queen. Clement VII fulminated against this situation and ordered Henry to return to Catherine, but he paid no attention. This left his former wife with nowhere to go, or rather it left her with the unacceptable option of receiving the designation 'Dowager Princess of Wales', with a consequent reduction in her status and establishment. The king imposed this solution upon her, and in the summer of 1533 her household was reorganised. This was not as drastic as might have been expected, but one of its consequences was the removal of a number of her ladies, including Jane Seymour.[6] It may be that Jane was considered to be unduly sympathetic to her mistress, or it may be that Henry had already spotted her, but she was transferred to the service of the new queen, and became a lady-in-waiting to Anne Boleyn.[7]

So, the Seymours were not a part of the Boleyn ascendancy, and the ease of this transfer remains something of a mystery. Sir Edward seems to have become an early protégé of Thomas Cromwell, who manoeuvred a number of financial deals with the Crown for him, and even paid one of his debts to the tune of £1,600 in September 1531.[8] Cromwell had clearly identified him as a coming man, although how far he had come is not clear. In exchanging New Year gifts with the king in 1532 he gave a jewelled sword, which Henry seems to have particularly appreciated. He had been appointed an Esquire of the Body in September 1531 as we have seen, and both Sir Edward and Sir John were in the royal entourage which went to Calais in October 1532. However, none of this suggests great intimacy, or the kind of influence which would have been needed to secure the transfer of his sister Jane to the chamber of the new queen. It may be that she had been put there for 're-education', but if so, someone clearly thought that she was worth converting, because Anne had a much more evangelical agenda than her predecessor.[9] Or it may be that her docility and irreproachable virginity marked her out as a girl who was not likely to cause any trouble. Since the last thing that Anne needed was competition, it may well be that she chose her herself. Her pedigree was not unlike that of the queen, and perhaps a certain empathy existed between them. Since Anne was accustomed to manage her own affairs, it may well be that no other patron need be sought, although Sir Edward's favour with the king may well have been a consideration.

One of her first duties in attendance upon the queen would have been to participate in the female mysteries of the laying-in. Anne took to her chamber in August 1533, and thereafter no male was supposed to intrude upon her presence until after the birth had taken place. This meant that all those tasks which normally fell to the Gentlemen Ushers and waiters, such as minding the door and waiting at table, now came to the queen's ladies. Female chamberers would also have performed those more menial tasks, like laying the fire, clearing away the ashes, and keeping the rooms clean, which otherwise would have been performed by the Grooms of the Chamber.[10] There is no evidence that Jane found any of these responsibilities onerous, and she took her turn with the others in sleeping on a pallet bed in the queen's bedroom. This last could have become a worrying responsibility as Anne's term approached, but at that time her place would probably have been taken by one of the royal midwives. We do not know very much about what happened at a queen's laying-in, because the women who knew did not talk about it, and the men who wrote the reports were not admitted. In the event the birth of Elizabeth, which occurred on 7 September, was uneventful, and there would have been little for Jane to do beyond carrying fresh supplies of water, and no doubt wine, when Her Majesty needed refreshment after her ordeal. The fact that the child was a girl was a bitter disappointment to both her parents, as well as to the astrologers who had confidently forecast a prince, and the subject of unseemly mirth around the courts of Europe. The King of England had broken with the Pope and brought his church and his immortal soul into peril for the sake of another daughter! Eustace Chapuys, the Imperial ambassador, could scarcely contain his satisfaction.[11]

Chapuys was, by virtue of his position, the implacable enemy of Anne, or 'the Concubine' as he insisted upon calling her. His brief was to defend the interests of Catherine, who was his master's kinswoman, and of her daughter Mary, by this time seventeen years old and as determined as her mother not to yield to the king's pressure. Elizabeth was christened on 10 September in the chapel of the Observant Franciscans at Greenwich, with Archbishop Cranmer as her godfather and the muted celebrations due to a princess. A few days later, at the end of the month, Mary's household was stood down and she was placed under virtual house arrest in the establishment created for her supplanter, the new Princess of England.[12] Chapuys was outraged by these proceedings, and began to seek what satisfaction he could find in the behaviour of the king. Henry had been deeply chagrined by the birth of his daughter, and did not attend her baptism, but it would be an exaggeration to say that he fell out with Anne in consequence. Together they put a brave front on the event. The queen was young and fertile and the boys would come. Within four months she was pregnant again, which does not suggest any breakdown in their relationship. Nevertheless, like most passionate marriages, this one had its ups and downs and Henry did not cease to pay his courtly attentions to the young ladies, who responded (for the most part) with enthusiasm.[13] Anne was not as complaisant as she should have been to these adventures, and as a result there were quarrels, which Chapuys assiduously tracked as a part of his campaign of vilification against her. However, for several months there was little substance to these stories of 'amours'. The royal couple regularly made up their rows with passionate reconciliations, and Chapuys was bound to admit that the concubine's influence was as great as it had ever been.[14]

However in June or July of 1534 Anne miscarried, and the king's demons began to return in earnest. He had been down this road many times with Catherine, and began to wonder whether he had been mistaken in taking a second wife. He had, however, made a heavy political investment in Anne, and if he allowed his doubts to appear in public, the pressure on him to return to Catherine and renegotiate his relations with the papacy would have become overwhelming. Chapuys had begun his insinuations a year before, before the birth of Elizabeth in fact, when he had reported an estrangement on 13 August 1533. However, he had been listening to gossip, and other evidence from the same period contradicts him completely.[15] In October, after the disappointment of Elizabeth, Henry was apparently making extravagant professions of affection for his wife, and according to Anne's ladies, declaring that he would beg alms from door to door rather than give her up. He kept his wife in touch with political affairs, and she helped him to whip opinion into line in preparation for the parliamentary session which was due in January 1534. If Jane had any sympathy with Mary at this point (and she probably had) she had the good sense to keep quiet about it. However, Anne's miscarriage made a crucial difference to the king's attitude, and at some point in August 1534 he appears to have begun an affair. According to Chapuys, writing in late September, Henry had had given up on the prospect of his wife having another child, and had 'renewed and increased the love that he had had previously toward another very beautiful maid of honour'.[16] Anne had reacted very badly and had wanted to dismiss the girl, but the king had reprimanded her, reminding her that she owed her position entirely to him, and that he was regretting the indulgence which he had shown her. A fortnight later he was reporting that Jane Rochford had been forbidden the court because she had been caught plotting with the queen to pick a quarrel with Henry's latest fancy, and force her to withdraw. The new lady was sending encouraging messages to Mary, saying that her troubles would soon be over, and Anne's influence was decreasing daily.[17] Many courtiers were alleged to be encouraging the king's fancy because of their desire to get rid of the concubine. Chapuys' dispatches were picked up in Rome, where the Imperial ambassador reported hearing the same stories. Anne's arrogance had led Henry to switch his attentions to someone else.[18]

That this someone else was Jane Seymour is pure speculation. When she does come on the scene in 1536 there is no reference to any previous relationship. Nor is the seriousness of the king's intentions by any means established. Chapuys' information came almost exclusively from Anne's enemies; for instance the story of her complaints in January 1534 came from Sir Nicholas Carew, and Jane Rochford is not noted to have been among her friends. The chances are that these stories in 1533 and 1534 were hopeful exaggerations of Henry's courtly love romances, which he is known to have pursued, and which had no ultimate significance.[19] Anne may well have objected to them, and the king been correspondingly annoyed, but the differences between them were short-lived, and did not signify any breakdown in the queen's position. They were lovers' quarrels, and Chapuys in his more rational moments recognised that perfectly well. Anne was nevertheless vulnerable in that she failed to make the critical transition from mistress to wife and mother. As Henry's mistress, she had been entitled to her fits of jealousy and pique if his eyes strayed to other women. She might be the darling of his heart, but she had to fight to retain that position, and she knew how to manage her royal lover.[20] She could also maintain an independent political position, provided that she did not cross him, and run her own businesses. Her tantrums consequently were calculated, and never failed to have their effect, bringing the king begging for forgiveness, and showering her with gifts. The worst that could have happened was that she would forfeit his affection, but she knew where to draw the line, and remained in control of the sexual exchanges between them. As a wife, however, her position was completely different. The wife of a king was expected to turn a blind eye to his 'affairs', to which he was by custom entitled, and Catherine had endured such treatment uncomplainingly for a number of years. She was also expected to be meek and submissive, not seeking to guide or advise her husband, and certainly not to pursue her own political agenda. None of this was consistent with Anne's character, and she was simply not a conventional queen.[21] Unfortunately Henry was an extremely conventional king, and expected her to make the necessary adjustments. When she failed to do so, their quarrels became more serious, and since she had only one weapon to retain his love, they tended to focus on his 'amours', real or imagined.

Apart from the physical aspect of their relationship, one other thing held them together. Catherine still lurked unhappily in the background, and as long as she lived Henry could not afford to admit that he had made a mistake over his second wife. Anne similarly was quite aware that her position as queen remained controversial in some quarters, and that many around the court remained secretly favourable to her predecessor. This meant that although she could upbraid Henry for his infidelities, she could not afford to go too far in case his whole attitude underwent a dramatic change, which was not likely, but could have happened. Chapuys made no secret of his partiality, and made it clear to the king that improved relations with the Emperor depended upon just such a change of heart.[22] He also made constant representations about Henry's treatment of Mary, seeking to use the king's affection for his daughter as means of driving the king and queen apart. He reported frequently on the hatred which Anne bore for Henry's daughter, and the ways in which she sought to motivate the king against her. If the 'concubine' had her way, Mary would have been faced with the Oath of Supremacy, and would have been executed for refusing to take it, but so far she had not prevailed.[23] How much the king knew of the contents of these reports we do not know, but he was well aware that the ambassador was trying to use Mary as a means of alienating Anne from her husband. That the fate of death awaited those who refused the Oath of Supremacy was demonstrated during the summer of 1535 by the executions of Sir Thomas More and Bishop John Fisher, but Henry would not allow the oath to be administered to Mary, or to Catherine. He did not want their blood on his hands as well.[24] Meanwhile his relationship with Anne continued to be up and down.

The king and queen spent most of the summer of 1535 on progress. They went across to the Severn, and then into Hampshire for most of September and October. Henry had not hunted the area for a number of years and the sport was good, particularly the hawking. He was no doubt glad to get away from London, and the aftermath of the executions. The people of the area gave him and Anne a cordial reception, which was no doubt gratifying, and he stopped at Winchester on 19 September to witness the consecration of three of his favourite clergy as bishops; Hugh Latimer to Worcester, John Hilsey to Rochester and Edward Fox to Hereford. Latimer was also a favourite of Anne's, and she was no doubt pleased by the whole event.[25] The royal couple appear to have been on relaxed terms throughout, and by the time that they returned to Windsor in late October, she was pregnant for the third time.[26] In the course of this perambulation, they stopped for several days in early September at Wolf Hall near Marlborough, the home of

Sir John Seymour and his numerous brood. In spite of later legend, it is by no means certain that Jane was present at this encounter, and if she was it was probably as one of the ladies accompanying the queen. We do not know who formed the entourage for the progress, and it is just as likely that Jane had been left behind in London. It is, however, very unlikely that she was in residence with her father awaiting the royal visitors, so the stories which declared that to be the first encounter between her and Henry are mistaken. She had, as we have seen, been around the court for a number of years, and although it is by no means established that he would have encountered her as one of Catherine's ladies, he knew her sufficiently well to bestow a New Year's gift on her in 1534, along with Anne Zouche, Madge Shelton and other members of Anne's chamber.[27] We do not know where Jane was in the summer and autumn of 1535, but if she was in London she was too wise to get involved in the demonstration in Mary's favour staged by a number of citizens' wives while the court was in Hampshire. Several court ladies were involved and Jane Rochford ended up in the Tower in consequence. The matter was hushed up, but it caused Henry to talk openly about his wife's pregnancy for the first time, as he tried to dampen down speculation about Mary's future in the event of his having no more children.[28]

Then, on 7 January 1536, Catherine died at Kimbolton and the political landscape was subtly changed. Henry reacted with relief; 'God be praised that we are now free from all suspicion of war'. The hostility of the Emperor could now be expected to abate, which would reduce his dependence upon France, and make Francis more amenable to his wishes.[29] He was also now free from any papal pressure to return to her, and Anne's position as queen would in future be unchallenged. There was an upsurge of enthusiasm for the Boleyns at court, and some even ventured to air the view that it was a pity that Mary had not followed her mother. Such thoughtless expressions naturally gave rise to speculation that Catherine had been poisoned, which Chapuys at first accepted, whereas it is clear from other evidence that she died from natural causes; probably a series of heart attacks. To Anne, however, her death was a mixed blessing. True, her position was now unchallenged; on the other hand should she fail for a third time to produce a son, it would be possible for the king to repudiate her without risk. If the child that she was carrying should prove to be male, and alive, then her position would be doubly assured, but if it turned out to be another daughter, she would be at the mercy of the next damsel to whom the king turned his affections. Meanwhile, such doubts were cast aside. The Sunday following the receipt of the news from Kimbolton, 9 January, the king and queen both appeared dressed in yellow, and the infant Elizabeth was triumphantly paraded to mass. In an apparent attempt to reassure his subjects of his continuing virility, the king, who had not jousted regularly for a number of years, ordered the lists to be prepared for a demonstration of his prowess. Then on 24 January, disaster struck. Henry's horse fell heavily in the lists at Greenwich and he was knocked unconscious for two hours.[30] All those who were aware of the accident held their breath, but the king quickly recovered, and apart from some very nasty bruises was none the worse. He did not attempt to joust again, and although that may have damaged his ego, at least he had been alerted to the fact that advancing years made such youthful exuberances inappropriate. Worse was to follow, because on the 29th Anne miscarried, blaming the news of his accident as the cause of her misfortune, although she must have received that at least four days earlier. Two descriptions of the foetus survive, which suggests the attendance of midwives, so the disaster cannot have been entirely unexpected, although otherwise the circumstances are not known. Both agree that it was male, and of about fifteen weeks' gestation, but do not mention any abnormality.[31] Many years later Nicholas Sander wrote that the foetus had been deformed and that had convinced the king that he could not be the father, which meant that his wife was guilty of adultery. But no contemporary evidence supports that interpretation, nor is there any recorded reaction from Henry except his extreme grief for the loss of another boy.[32] He was probably still recovering from the battering which he had received in the lists at Greenwich. Within a few days, however, doubts of the old kind had resurfaced. It had been her failure to bear him a son, and her repeated miscarriages, which had convinced him that his first marriage had offended against the law of God. Could it be that he had offended again in his second marriage? If so, it was obviously not in the same way, and he was at a loss to account for it, but God was clearly punishing him by denying him a son. He began to think of the possibility of repudiating Anne and starting again. In February 1536 it was no more than a thought, but it communicated itself to Thomas Cromwell and the secretary began to consider his options.[33]

At the same time, and possibly as a result, Henry began to be seriously interested in Jane Seymour. Chapuys reported this 'new amour' on 18 March and wrote that he had described Henry's infatuation with the young lady before, but now it had become serious, 'to the rage of the concubine'. The descriptions which he referred to were recent, and it does not seem that he associated Jane with the anonymous young lady of 1534. Now, however, he knew who she was.[34] A fortnight earlier, Thomas Cromwell had been displaced from a chamber which he occupied next to the king's, and Sir Edward Seymour and his wife had been installed. This chamber would have been a suit of rooms in the most prestigious part of Greenwich Palace, and was connected with the royal apartments by a secret passage. Sir Edward had just been appointed as a Gentleman of the Privy Chamber, and therefore might have merited such accommodation in his own right, but Chapuys speculated, no doubt correctly, that the arrangement was designed to facilitate communications with his sister, Jane, who could have visited her brother without provoking any comment from the watchful courtiers. Cromwell, who knew the king's mind, no doubt gave up his chamber willingly, and if Anne, who also knew what was going on, was as angry as Chapuys suggests, then she was digging a hole for herself. However, he tells contradictory stories.[35] At one point he was claiming that Henry had hardly spoken to Anne for three months, and at another that he was upset by her expressions of devotion and went off to spend Shrovetide (28 February) on his own at Whitehall instead of celebrating with her at Greenwich. That the king was at Westminster for Shrovetide is confirmed from other sources, but there could have been good reasons for that, apart from his annoyance with Anne. There was urgent business being transacted in the parliament at that juncture, which demanded his presence, and the queen was probably still convalescent after her miscarriage. Since Chapuys is our main source for these developments, and he had his own agenda, it would be unwise to conclude that Henry had already decided as early as the end of February to abandon Anne and take a third wife.[36]

Many stories were later told of the final breakdown of the royal marriage, but they were mostly written years after the event and depended upon hearsay evidence of the most unreliable kind. One typical example is that derived from Jane Dormer in the early seventeenth century. Jane was not even born at the time of the alleged exchanges, and derived her information from one of Anne's ladies, reminiscing in old age. According to this account, it had been catching Henry and Jane *in flagrante delicto* which had caused the queen to miscarry, and she had upbraided him bitterly: 'See how well I must be since the day I caught that abandoned woman Jane sitting on your knee.'

There had been 'much scratching and bye blows between the queen and her maid' as a result, but the king would not permit her to dismiss the errant Jane, so the bad feeling continued.[37] Such stories have all the hallmarks of hindsight, and Henry was in fact referring in all apparent sincerity to his 'entirely beloved wife' in public as late as the end of April. Although his mind was prepared for the contingency, his decision to proceed against Anne for adultery seems to have been a sudden one, taken, probably, on 1 May. The king was literally bounced into a decision by Thomas Cromwell on the evidence of her exchanges with Sir Henry Norris.[38] Meanwhile, Henry had apparently made an attempt on Jane's virtue. Chapuys reported this on 1 April, on the evidence of one 'Gelyot', who may have been Sir Thomas Elyot, a Gentleman of the Privy Chamber. Henry, so the story goes, was at Westminster, and 'the young lady whom he serves, Mrs Semel', at Greenwich. The king sent her a purse full of sovereigns and a letter. We do not know what the letter contained, but it was probably a proposition similar to that which Henry had offered to Anne in the spring of 1527. Jane obviously suspected such matter, because having kissed the letter, she returned it to the messenger unopened,

> and then, throwing herself on her knees before him, begged the said messenger that he would pray the king on her part to consider that she was a gentlewoman of good and honourable parents, without reproach, and that she had no greater treasure in the world than her honour, which she would rather die a thousand deaths than tarnish...[39]

If the king was minded to send her a present of money, then she begged that he would do so once God had sent her a good match. She presumably returned the purse of sovereigns also on this occasion, although Chapuys is silent on that point. There is something theatrical and artificial about this display of virtue, as though Jane, like Anne before her, was angling for the bigger prize, and was aware of her advantage over the queen. The king, we are told, was duly impressed, and declared rather oddly that henceforth he would speak to her only in the presence of some member of her family. It may be presumed that this statement was for public consumption, at least within the Privy Chamber, and was designed to dampen down speculation. There is no reason to suppose that Henry abided by it.[40]

Jane would have been well informed about Privy Chamber gossip and of her own place in it. She would also have been aware that Mary's friends were rallying to her, as her chances of unseating the queen seemed to grow during April. How large a part the king's affection for Jane played in Anne's ultimate downfall we do not know, nor whether Mary's friends were significantly involved. The crucial person in this situation was Thomas Cromwell, who had fallen out with the queen towards the end of March over his intention (and the king's) to take the property of the smaller monasteries into royal hands.[41] On Passion Sunday (2 April), John Skip, who was Anne's almoner, preached openly against such a policy in the Chapel Royal, citing the Old Testament story of Haman and Ahasuerus, and of the latter's intention to massacre the Jews. 'There was a good woman (which this gentle king Ahasuerus loved very well and put his trust in because he knew that she was ever his friend) and she gave the king contrary counsel', with the result that the Jews were saved and Haman was hanged. No one in the chapel could have missed the allusion. Ahasuerus was Henry VIII, his 'good woman' Esther was Anne, and Haman was Thomas Cromwell.[42] Anne was fighting back, but the king was not amused and Cromwell was more alienated than before. For the time being, Boleyn influence remained strong in the court, but by the end of April the king's attitude (which was the only one which really mattered) had come to a knife-edge. Cromwell, meanwhile, had fed another notion into Henry's uncertain mind. If his second marriage was invalid, how was his long pursuit of Anne to be explained? One possible explanation lay in witchcraft; Anne had bewitched her unsuspecting partner into his long infatuation. This had the great advantage of absolving the king from responsibility; it also made her descent into adultery more plausible, because that was what witches did.[43] Then on 29 or 30 April Anne had a furious altercation with Sir Henry Norris, in which she accused him of wanting to possess her 'if ought but good should happen to the king'. Word of this row was all over the court in a matter of hours. It was treason to imagine the death of the king, and taken to be evidence of their earlier sexual relationship.[44] Cromwell acted fast, and later in the day on the 30th Mark Smeaton, a musician who had been pining after Anne for some time, was arrested and charged with adultery with her. These developments finally made up Henry's mind, and on 2 May Anne was arrested and taken to the Tower.

While Anne was in custody and awaiting the attentions of the Earl Marshall's court, the king turned to Jane, and he had her removed to a house belonging to Sir Nicholas Carew, which was more conveniently situated for visits from Westminster than was Greenwich. There he paid court to her, while Anne became a non-person. Condemned of treason by the Court of Peers, she forfeited her title as Marquis of Pembroke by virtue of her attainder, and a few days later her marriage was declared null and void by the Archbishop's Court which had previously endorsed it. The cause papers for this hearing do not survive, so we cannot be sure of the grounds for this change of heart. It cannot have been the adultery, which was alleged to have taken place later, and must have been to do with the consanguinity which resulted from Henry's earlier liaison with her sister Mary, although that had been known about in 1533.[45] The real reason for the decision, however, was that the king would have it so. Anne was executed on 19 May, and the following morning, Henry proposed to Jane and was accepted. This betrothal was intended to be a secret, because it was undoubtedly a hasty action on the king's part, but it became known almost at once, giving support to the popular notion that it was desire for Jane which had fuelled the king's intention to have his second wife beheaded. As we have seen, such an explanation was too simple, and it was probably Cromwell who decided initially that the queen must die. Of course he had to persuade the king, but it would have been his ascendancy which she could have continued to threaten had she been shunted into retirement as Catherine had been. She was simply too good a politician to be allowed to survive, and the same applied to her brother George, who was executed on even feebler evidence for alleged incest with her. To secure the secretary's position, the whole Boleyn clan had to be destroyed.[46]

The courts of Europe were fascinated by this spectacle. The King of England would simply stop at nothing to gratify his lust. On 18 May, Chapuys wrote to Cardinal Granvelle, sending him a description of the woman who was now likely to be England's next queen.

> She is sister to one Edward Seymour, the king's man, of middle stature and no great beauty, so fair that one would call her pale rather than otherwise. She is now over twenty-five years old, and I leave it to you to judge whether being English and having long frequented the court she has an advantage...[47]

He hesitated whether to describe her as intelligent or not, but she carried no political baggage, and he added shrewdly, 'Perhaps the king will be only too glad to be so far relieved from trouble.' Jane apparently had no agenda of her own, and no desire apart from pleasing the king, which she was well-equipped to do. Two days later he wrote again, saying that he had just been informed that the betrothal had taken place at 9 o'clock that morning, Mistress Seymour having come secretly to the king's lodgings by river.[48] Henry had wished to keep it secret until Whitsun (4 June), but everyone was talking about it 'and saying that before the death of the other there was some arrangement, which seems ill in the eyes of the people...'

The only people who could have known about the betrothal at that point would have been courtiers, but the statement was also true in more general terms, because Anne's treatment, which had been very public, had raised many eyebrows. It is ironic that Anne's only experience of public sympathy came over the manner of her death. Even Chapuys, her bitter enemy, was puzzled by it, and Jane consequently became the 'other woman' who was credited with the queen's downfall. She thus began her public career as the putative friend of the Lady Mary, and it remained to be seen whether that was an advantage or not. She was also in another sense a client of the all-powerful secretary, Thomas Cromwell.

3

A WHIRLWIND ROMANCE

The suddenness of Anne Boleyn's fall caught the courts of Europe off balance. Since Catherine's death the Emperor had been considering the possibility of reviving his alliance with Henry VIII, and had even persuaded Chapuys to be polite to Anne when they had encountered in the Chapel Royal.[1] In this he was undoubtedly encouraged by Thomas Cromwell, who did not trust the French, or the alliance with Francis which the Boleyn ascendancy represented. Given the opportunity, Charles would probably have suggested an Imperial bride for the now-widowed king as a means to that end. Pope Paul III, convinced that Anne had been the cause of the schism, looked forward to a new negotiation. However, the speed of Henry's reaction defeated all speculation. As we have seen, Chapuys was in a position to inform Cardinal Granvelle of the king's betrothal on the very day that it had happened, and ten days later he was able to report that his forecast had been accurate; Henry had taken 'Mrs Semel' to wife.[2] The ambassador had no great opinion of his choice, although it is doubtful if he had much first-hand experience of her; she was, he wrote, 'of no great wit' and was reported to be proud and haughty. However, she had one great redeeming feature in his eyes; she was friendly towards 'the princess', and her influence with the king might well bring about a reconciliation between them. On 30 May, Henry and Jane were quietly married in the queen's closet at Whitehall, and a few days later the new queen made her first attempt to persuade the king of the merits of his estranged daughter. She was told (gently it would seem) to mind her own business.[3] On 3 June Sir John Russell wrote to Lord Lisle that on the previous day Jane had been 'shown to the court' as queen, and continued,

> I assure you she is as gentle a lady as ever I knew, and as fair a queen as any in Christendom. The king has come out of hell into heaven for the gentleness of this and the cursedness and unhappiness of the other...[4]

Lisle would be well-advised to write his congratulations to Henry as soon as possible; and on 6 June, after mass, the Imperial ambassador was invited to accompany the royal couple to the queen's chamber when 'for the king's satisfaction' he kissed her and congratulated her upon her marriage. The Emperor would, he said, be delighted to know that the king had found so good and virtuous a wife, especially as her brother had once been in the Emperor's service. 'The satisfaction of the people with this marriage,' he added, 'is incredible.'[5]

The practicalities of the new situation were soon resolved. Parliament, which convened on 8 June, passed a new Act confirming the illegitimacy of both Mary and Elizabeth, and settling the succession on any child born to the present queen, or to any future spouse whom the king might wed. Other statutes confirmed the queen's jointure, which consisted largely of lands taken over from the late Anne, to the tune of about £3,000 a year, and the gift of Paris Garden in London, which the king had made over to Jane a few days earlier.[6] On 5 June her brother Edward was created Viscount Beauchamp, a title which had been dredged out of his family history, and on 1 July took his oath as a member of the king's council. A rumour quickly spread that he had been appointed Lord Privy Seal in succession to the Earl of Wiltshire, but whereas Wiltshire had certainly been dismissed, his replacement was Thomas Cromwell, appointed on 29 June. The chief minister had no intention of allowing so substantial a fruit of his victory over the Boleyns to be bestowed elsewhere. Perhaps as a consolation, Edward Seymour was granted the office of Governor and Captain of Jersey just a few days later.[7] He seems to have taken his responsibilities there seriously, but worked through deputies. He may have visited the Channel Islands, but there is no evidence that he ever lived there; he was too preoccupied with the life of the court. He was also appointed Chancellor of North Wales on 16 August, but there is no suggestion that he went there either. Meanwhile his financial dispute with Lord Lisle continued. His agent – one Hollys – would not grant any respite on the payments due, so John Hussee persuaded Cromwell to write to Viscount Beauchamp on Lisle's behalf, but even this appeal was apparently in vain. To be fair to Seymour, his own affairs were probably not in the best of shape at that time, because on 21 July he features on a list of lords and ladies who had defaulted on the last payment of the subsidy, which was not the best of ways to retain the favour which he was then enjoying.[8] He also owed Lisle money, which he apparently agreed to pay through Cromwell as intermediary, but according to other letters of Hussee in November, that did not work either. At the end of the month they were still trying to get the money out of him.[9]

Another piece of outstanding business was the question of the queen's Coronation. Both Catherine and Anne had been crowned, and it was naturally supposed that a similar honour would be bestowed upon Henry's new queen. When John Hussee wrote to Lady Lisle, on 18 September, as he frequently did on domestic business, he not only conveyed the queen's best wishes but announced that her Coronation would take place on the Sunday 'next after All Hallows', which would have been 5 November.

Where he got this precise information from is not clear, but when early November came, the king was much preoccupied with the northern rising, and the event was postponed. It was not, however, cancelled, and there was considerable speculation in diplomatic circles that it would not take place until Jane had proved her worth by becoming a mother. There was naturally much interest in the queen's condition, one ill-informed commentator reporting as early as 26 June that 'the King of England has married a lady who is six months pregnant by him', which may well have been a transferred memory of his wedding to Anne Boleyn just over three years earlier.[10] The commentator was based in Rome, and clearly did not have the benefit of Chapuys' more accurate information. Meanwhile, there was the vexed question of Henry's relationship with his daughter. Jane, as we have seen, was reputed to be friendly towards Mary, and within days of their wedding had been urging reconciliation upon the king, on the grounds that Anne, who had been her great enemy, was now gone. Henry, however, was unconvinced. A few days before his crisis with Anne, he had told Chapuys,

> As to the legitimation of our daughter Mary ... if she would submit to our Grace without wrestling against the determination of our laws, we would acknowledge her and use her as our daughter, but we would not be directed or pressed therein...[11]

In other words he was looking for an unconditional submission, and the presence or absence of Anne was irrelevant. Mary did not understand this; as far as she was concerned, Anne's fall changed everything, and throughout May 1536 she waited for the initiative from her father which would spell forgiveness. The misapprehension was a common one, shared according to Chapuys by both the common people and by Queen Jane. They did not want to realise what Cromwell understood perfectly well; that the king was totally committed to his ecclesiastical supremacy, and would not make any move which compromised that independence. So throughout May and the early part of June Mary waited, while her erstwhile servants started turning up at Hunsdon, expecting to be reinstated.[12] However, Elizabeth's status was now as indeterminate as Mary's, and Chapuys advised Lady Shelton, who had charge of the establishment, not to take on anyone without the king's express authorisation. On 26 May Mary wrote to Cromwell, asking also for his intercession now that the woman who had alienated her from her father was gone. The secretary replied promptly, as was his wont, informing her that obedience was looked for as the condition of reinstatement, but Mary did not read the signal. On the 30th she wrote again, offering to be as 'obedient to the king's grace as you can reasonably require of me'. Without waiting for a response to this piece of alarming innocence, she wrote directly to her father, acknowledging her offences and begging his blessing 'in as humble and lowly a manner as possible'. She congratulated him upon his recent marriage, and asked for leave to wait upon the new queen.[13] Unfortunately she also made it clear that there were limits to her submissiveness. She would obey her father in all things 'next to God', begging him to remember that she had committed herself to the Almighty, and that the ecclesiastical supremacy and her mother's marriage were 'off limits' as far as obedience was concerned. Because she was therefore offering nothing new, the king did not even trouble to reply, but rather went ahead and drew up a set of articles to be presented to her, which would allow no room for equivocation. Cromwell was on tenterhooks, because it was no part of his plan to see the princess executed for high treason. He drew up a letter of submission for her to sign, and took Chapuys into his confidence. On 6 June the latter reported that he could see an honourable way out of the impasse, but that seems to have been short of signing the letter. He may have communicated this false optimism to Mary, because on the

7th she wrote to Cromwell, asking for some token of forgiveness before she paid her anticipated visit to the court, and on the 8th to Henry expressing her joy that he had withdrawn his displeasure.[14] Sadly this was premature, and did not merit any reply. Instead on about the 15th the king sent a commission, headed by the Duke of Norfolk, to Hunsdon to demand an unequivocal answer to two questions: would she accept his ecclesiastical supremacy, and the annulment of her parents' marriage, or not? After a stormy and emotional confrontation, she rejected both demands, and thereby exposed herself to the penalties of high treason. The crisis which Cromwell and Chapuys had dreaded was now upon them.[15] The council went into emergency session to decide what to do about her, and it must have been at about that time that Queen Jane took a hand. She wrote to Mary, probably advising her to submit on the ground that such cruel pressure would surely absolve her conscience. On 21st the princess replied, thanking her for her 'most prudent counsel', and begging her intercession for an interview with her father. Within a few days she had signed Cromwell's letter of submission and the crisis was over. Chapuys represented her as conscience-smitten by her surrender, but other evidence suggests a sudden relaxation of the tension of the previous weeks, which was probably as much of a relief to Henry as it was to her.[16] On 6 July the king and queen visited Hunsdon and stayed for two days, during which time the affection between the two women seems to have blossomed.

How important Jane's intervention in this crisis was remains a matter for speculation, because her letter to Mary does not survive, but the nature of the princess's response suggests what form her good counsel must have taken. It was the kind of advice which either Chapuys or Cromwell could have offered, and the former certainly did so, but it seems to have been Jane's kindly and 'motherly' concern which tipped the balance in Mary's mind. Their relationship thereafter can be shown to have been warm and cordial. Nothing was said about the succession, and rumours that Mary would be created Duchess of York turned out to be groundless. Nevertheless her Chamber was reconstituted within a matter of weeks, and she re-entered the marriage market. The emperor was still keen to match her with Dom Luis, the son of the King of Portugal, as a means of cementing a new relationship with England.[17] However, it was in the direction of France that Henry took an initiative, writing on 12 July to his agents there instructing them to offer her legitimation and inclusion in the succession in return for an undertaking that the Duke of Angoulême, Francis' third son, would wed her and reside for part of the time in England. How serious he was about these plans, which run counter to so many previous statements, is hard to gauge. Mary did not take them very seriously, but they did signify that she was back on the market after three years in the wilderness, and that in itself was a matter of some importance. Meanwhile sorrow had once again clouded the king's joy in his wife's company, because on 23 July the seventeen-year-old Duke of Richmond died, probably of pneumonia.[18] Chapuys was quite clear that Henry had intended to name him as his heir, failing male issue by Jane, but there is no supporting evidence for such a conclusion. His death did, however, highlight Mary's position still further. Legitimate or not, she was the king's eldest child, and must have succeeded him if he had died in the autumn of 1536. Only Queen Jane could stand between that undesirable outcome and its recognition, and it is therefore natural that the court watchers were exceedingly anxious to detect any signs of pregnancy in her. However, for the time being they had to be content with the fact that the royal couple were 'merry' together, and as far as Henry was concerned, his honeymoon extended well into the autumn. On 12 July the king instructed Archbishop Cranmer to include the queen in the bidding prayers, and on the 18th parliament passed the Act vesting the succession in the heirs of her body.[19] It still remained for her to perform that feat however, and by October there were signs of anxiety about the court gossip.

By then Henry needed his domestic harmony, because his realm was out of sorts. There was widespread discontent over the dissolution of the smaller monasteries, and over his evangelical policies in general, and on 2 October the men of Louth and Horncastle in Lincolnshire rose in rebellion. At least, that was the way it looked in London. On 7 October a list was drawn up of those nobles and gentlemen who were to go against the 'northern rebels'; there were about 100 of them and Viscount Beauchamp features fifth on the list, which was surely a mark of the trust placed in him.[20] He was supposed to raise 200 men, and may indeed have done so although they did not march against the Lincolnshire rebels. This was partly because the Lincolnshire men did not see themselves as rebels at all, and professed the warmest loyalty to the king. In their own eyes they were making a protest against 'evil councillors', particularly Cromwell and Cranmer, and had no agenda which involved deposing Henry. The demonstration was primarily a movement of the commons, and was largely stirred up by conservative clergy, but it also involved the taking and recruitment to the cause of a substantial number of local gentry. Apparently they felt the need of 'natural' leaders, but how committed these gentlemen were to the cause which they ostensibly led may be doubted.[21] Nevertheless within ten days they had raised almost 20,000 men and occupied Lincoln without any kind of resistance. The question then arose as to what to do next, because a herald reached Lincoln bearing a conciliatory message from the king, and it was felt that to advance further would be unnecessary provocation. It was decided to send a representative to London, seeking Henry's reassurance that the rumours of the confiscation of church goods, which had helped to trigger the movement, were unfounded, and also a modification of the taxation demands which had been another major cause of the uprising. At the same time, and probably in the same connection, a series of articles were drawn up, addressed to 'the king our sovereign lord'. These started with what was ostensibly the main grievance – the dissolution of the monasteries.[22]

> The suppression of so many religious houses as are at this instant time suppressed, whereby the service of our God is not well [maintained] but also the commons of your realm unrelieved the which as we think is a great hurt to the commonwealth...

They then proceeded to complain of the Statute of Uses, the tax or quindene of 4d for every beast, 'the which would be an importable charge to them (the commons) considering the poverty they be in already', and of the king's use of base-born councillors, particularly Cromwell and Richard Rich. The document concluded with a protest against the appointment of certain named bishops who were suspected of being behind the king's religious policies, including (oddly enough) the conservative Bishop of Lincoln, John Longland. The Statute of Uses was a gentleman's grievance, but apart from that this document no doubt reflected the commons' complaints fairly enough.[23] It was also a means of buying time for both sides, and by the time that the king's response reached Lincoln, the gentlemen had persuaded their followers to go home. The Lincolnshire revolt, in spite of its formidable appearance, therefore fizzled out after about a fortnight, and the gentlemen who had been involved hastened to submit to the Duke of Suffolk, who was in command of such forces as the king had been able to raise, and were on the whole favourably received. Reassured that there was no longer any threat from the county, the king's formal response, when it arrived in Lincoln, was far from conciliatory, taking the protesters to task for daring to lecture their king about what he should and should not do, or whom he should consult. They were, he went on, merely the inhabitants of one of the most 'brutish' shires in the realm, nor were the gentlemen as 'whole' as they pretended to be.[24] It is doubtful whether this alarming communication reached more than a handful of those at whom it was aimed, but it did not really matter. A selection of the ringleaders of the revolt were rounded up, tried and executed, but there was no further trouble from Lincolnshire, where the natural order of gentry authority was quickly restored, and with one or two exceptions the role of the gentlemen in leading the movement was quietly forgotten.

However, before the Lincolnshire rising collapsed in the second week of October, its message had been communicated across the Humber into the East Riding of Yorkshire, and the commons rose in a similar fashion, with the clergy taking the initiative. This self-styled Pilgrimage of Grace spread rapidly into other parts of Yorkshire, and quickly adopted a more radical agenda. Here the protests were headed by complaints against the heresies of Luther, Wycliffe and Melanchthon, with the demand that they be exterminated, and against the Royal Supremacy, asking that ecclesiastical jurisdiction be returned to the Pope. These were then followed by a demand that the Princess Mary be reinstated as legitimate; and the dissolution of the abbeys came only as the fourth clause.[25] Lincolnshire had not mentioned the Supremacy, nor Mary, nor heresy, although that could be construed from their protest at the bishops. So the Yorkshire Pilgrimage represented a threat that was both more thoughtful and more fundamental; a repudiation, in fact, of royal policy over the previous five years. This agenda it probably owed to Robert Aske, a lawyer and dependant of the Percies, who quickly assumed a leading role. The issue of the abbeys may be taken as representative of his leadership, because it was an issue upon which he felt strongly.[26] Henry's policy on the abbeys was controversial, even among those who supported the Royal Supremacy, and might have been thought to be negotiable. Queen Anne had opposed it, not out of any tenderness towards monks, but because she felt that the proceeds should have been used to build the church rather than diverted to purely secular purposes. Queen Jane also opposed it, and the story began to circulate that she had gone down on her knees in an attempt to persuade her husband to spare the abbeys, all to no avail, because the king's conscience seems to have been genuinely touched by the issue. He needed the money, there is no doubt about that, and he used the lands to reward those of his subjects whom he considered to be the most deserving, including the Seymour brothers, but that does not seem to have been his primary objective.[27] It seems that he had a genuine aversion to the religious orders, which stemmed from his youthful admiration for Erasmus. They were, he thought, idle and corrupt, and the small houses were the worst of them all. In fact, although not all the small houses were dens of vice, many which had fewer than a dozen inmates found it hard to discharge their liturgical obligations, and even harder to support the hospitality and education which were among their secondary purposes. He therefore supported Cromwell's Bill for the dissolution of houses with incomes of less than £200 a year, which passed in the summer of 1536.[28] The Pilgrims might complain that without them God was not properly served nor hospitality maintained, but the reports of Henry's commission of enquiry reveal that this was often special pleading. There was a genuine case for this dissolution, although Anne (and Archbishop Cranmer) were no doubt right in arguing that the proceeds could have been better bestowed. However the Act of Parliament made provision for the continuance of the major houses, 'divers great and solemn monasteries of this realm, wherein, thanks be to God, religion is right well kept and observed', which would also house those members of the dissolved houses who wished to continue their vocation.[29] Whether this represents the *quid pro quo* which Cromwell judged necessary to get his Bill through the Lords or a genuine ambiguity in the king's conscience is not apparent. If it was the latter, then Henry quickly yielded to the logic of events, because the pressure rapidly built up on the greater houses to surrender also, and they did so one by one over the following four years. Queen Jane may well have been genuinely distressed by this turn of events, but she made no further protest, or at least not that anyone reported. As early as 20 September 1536 Martin Luther noted that 'according to Alesius' the new Queen of England was an enemy of the gospel, and that as a result of her influence Robert Barnes had gone into hiding.[30] However, the convocation of 1536 had also passed the theologically ambiguous Ten Articles, which the king seems to have perused with some care, so Luther was probably using 'the gospel' as a shorthand for his own theological position, which Henry certainly continued to reject. The king's conscience continued to go its own way, and his subjects, including his wife, had to make the best of it.

Or not, in the case of the Pilgrimage of Grace. The Pilgrims spread their message around Yorkshire and into Cumbria with incredible rapidity, and swept together a number of separate and spontaneous protests. The motivation for these ranged widely, and many were about local issues; bad landlords, or neo-feudal loyalties which bound tenants to their disaffected lords, or border tenures.[31] However, religious discontents were general and appealed to all the various constituencies which made up the movement. Aske may have had as many as 30,000 men under his command when he advanced to Pontefract in early December. Meanwhile the Duke of Norfolk had been appointed Royal Lieutenant, with commission to negotiate with the rebels, a strategy which Henry had been compelled to adopt because of the paucity of the force which he could place at Norfolk's disposal. Throughout the crisis the king continued to be ebullient, never apparently doubting his ability to crush the rising, but for a number of weeks the evidence was against him. Eventually his confidence was justified, but that was because the northern men, like those of Lincolnshire, saw themselves as protesters, not rebels.[32] Although Aske had so many men at Pontefract, ostensibly for the same purpose, they were in fact riven with disagreements; divided both in their leadership and in their objectives. There were also problems involved in leading so many men so far from their homes, and they were being held together with great difficulty by a mixture of local leadership and a common sense of purpose. Consequently Aske may not have had a very difficult task in persuading even the more hot-headed of the leaders to accept his plan for negotiation. These took place in a number of different stages. Before the Lincolnshire rising had collapsed, Henry had ordered musters at Ampthill, and placed the Duke of Norfolk in command, and since the news from the north arrived before it was certain that Lincoln was pacified, that force was mobilised at the end of October and instructed to accompany the duke on his new mission. He therefore had about 7,000 men when he encountered the rebels for the first time at Doncaster. The Earl of Shrewsbury was already in the north with a rather smaller force but even if they had worked together they would still not have been strong enough to defeat the rebels in the field, and therefore Norfolk also agreed to negotiate.[33] After the first encounter, the duke sent a conciliatory message to the Pilgrims' Council at York, intended to persuade them that all was well, and that they could go home while the king addressed their grievances. Aske, however, was not deceived by these blandishments, having seen what had happened in Lincolnshire, and kept his host in being in spite of the growing difficulties of doing so during a phase of inactivity. The leaders of the Pilgrimage debated long and earnestly over the nature of the articles which they should present to Norfolk, while the threat of force still lurked in the background. They realised that an instant response to two long and complex documents (one for the clergy and one for the laity) was not likely, and therefore concentrated their demands on two points; a free general pardon, and a parliament to meet in the north to resolve those issues which required legislation. When the meeting took place on 6 December, Norfolk, acting under instructions from the king, professed that his commission did not extend so far, and sought a few days' delay while he consulted Henry.[34] In fact this was a mere ruse, because the promise of such a pardon already existed in the hands of Sir John Russell and was with the king's lieutenant almost at once. Had the Pilgrims demanded more, he was to secure a longer truce on whatever pretext he chose in order to give the government time to build up its forces to a level at which they could reasonably confront them. As it turned out, such a delay was not necessary, because Aske and his colleagues accepted the king's offer of a pardon and a parliament, and when the former was read out, he solemnly took off his Pilgrims badge of the five wounds of Christ, declaring that he would henceforth wear no badge or sign 'but the badge of our sovereign lord'.[35] On this understanding the Pilgrims eventually dispersed, on Aske's instructions, and he himself went to court to negotiate the implementation of what had ostensibly been agreed.

Although he implicitly confirmed what Norfolk had negotiated on his behalf, it is very doubtful whether Henry had any intention of abiding by it. He had only promised a pardon, and undertaken to summon a parliament to York at some indeterminate date in the future. Some understanding also seems to have been reached about the future of the monasteries, although what that was we cannot be sure because the duke's letter to Henry, outlining the agreement, is now missing.[36] The king was buying time while he built up his own forces, which went on increasing after the Doncaster agreement, and it seems to have been his intention to reduce the north to obedience by force. In the event his dissimulation was justified, up to a point, by the outbreak of fresh risings in Yorkshire and Cumberland in February 1537. Sir Francis Bigod, a religious reformer whose agenda had nothing to do with the original Pilgrimage, raised a force and attacked the town of Hull. At the same time the commons of Cumberland and Westmorland laid siege to Carlisle. Neither of these movements remotely resembled the power of the Pilgrimage proper, and were suppressed by royal forces without difficulty. However they gave the king an excuse to renege on his promises, and he exacted a bloody revenge.[37] Aske, Lord Darcy and the other original leaders had not been a party to these new insurrections but were nevertheless rounded up, put on trial and executed. By mid-May the Duke of Norfolk had also descended on Yorkshire and executed a select number of those responsible for the original rising on the grounds that the king's pardon was now null and void. Henry's severity can be justified by looking at the international implications, because the king stood under sentence of excommunication, and the Pope was looking for whatever leverage he could obtain against him. As soon as news of the rising reached Rome, Paul III created Reginald Pole a cardinal and dispatched him on a mission of support for the rebels. He was to call upon Henry to return to the fold, and if he refused, to mobilise either the Emperor or the King of France against him.[38] It was a forlorn hope, because both Francis and Charles were more concerned to obtain Henry's alliance than to end the English schism, and in any case it was mid-February before Pole reached Northern Europe. The main rising was long since over, and the cleaning-up operations were well under way. He did not have the money to raise mercenaries himself, and there was nothing that he could do, beyond convincing the king that he was a double-dyed traitor.

Mary featured largely in the Pontefract articles, but there was no suggestion that she had consented to the use of her name. She remained quietly at court, developing her friendship with Jane and occupying second place among the ladies, after the queen. In March 1537 she even wrote to the Emperor, asking him not to use her as a means of applying pressure to her father, as he had done through Chapuys in recent years. She was, she professed, completely reconciled in her conscience to her father's supremacy and her own illegitimacy.[39] Charles was not pleased, suspecting (no doubt rightly) that these letters were prompted by Henry, but since he had no intention of intervening against him, the only tangible result was a certain chill in his relations with Mary. Lord Hussey, her former steward, was one of those executed for his part in the rising, but no one suggested that she was implicated. The Emperor could not bring himself to believe that her change of heart was genuine, but was relieved by her restoration to favour. As early as February he began to press John III of Portugal to make a firm offer of a marriage with Dom Luis, and John gave his ambassador in London full powers to negotiate such a match, but nothing came of it because Henry was unwilling to concede her legitimacy and her place in the succession.[40] By March he may well have been suspecting that his wife was pregnant, and he wanted nothing to confuse the right of that child, as established by the Act of the previous summer. The negotiations dragged on until June, when Henry finally killed them by suggesting that any resulting treaty would have to be confirmed by parliament. The Portuguese went away, and how disappointed Mary may have been we do not know. The best that could be said for a Portuguese match would have been that it would have protected her against disparagement.[41] Whether Jane played any part in these negotiations we do not know. It would have been characteristic of her to be concerned for her friend's happiness, but we know very little of Mary's own attitude, and no one thought to comment on the queen's. What can be reasonably deduced is that she would have exerted herself in favour of a peaceful solution to the northern crisis. She would have played a part in welcoming Robert Aske to the court over the Christmas season, but apparently when in early December she had ventured to tell the king that God had permitted the insurrection to take place because of the 'razing' of so many churches, he told her, as he had before, to mind her own business.[42] On 23 December she accompanied the king on a parade through London, which seems to have been intended to raise the monarch's profile, and on the 31st John Hussee reported to Lord Lisle that she would be crowned at York, after the parliament which was due to be held there.[43] Whether Hussee's sources were misinformed or Henry was still giving out this kind of information at that date is not known. It would have been reasonable to have linked the Coronation to a parliament, but other sources suggest that he never had any intention of honouring that part of his agreement with the Pilgrims. Meanwhile the absence of any sign of pregnancy in Jane was causing dark mutterings among the people. On 18 January it was reported from Rutland that it was being said that 'the king used too many women to be able to get a child of his queen'.[44] The logic of such statements is hard to grasp, but Henry clearly had a sexual reputation which did not at all correspond to the facts. As far as we know, he never looked at another woman throughout his marriage to Jane, and even his courtly love adventures seem to have been curtailed. At least no one who was in a position to know commented upon his 'amours' during this period. He seems to have become completely uxorious, or it may be that his energies were flagging. He was forty-six, and had confided to Cromwell at one point that he doubted whether he would ever have children by Jane. The news of her pregnancy, which was confirmed by the end of March, must therefore have come as a huge relief to him. By the summer of 1537 Henry was therefore in good form. He had seen off the threat of the Pilgrimage, and punished the leaders to his satisfaction; Pole's mission had turned out to be a fiasco, and his wife was expecting a child.

4

JANE THE QUEEN

At the beginning of 1537 the Duke of Norfolk returned to the north. On 1 February he was at Doncaster, where he was greeted by a number of the local gentry, who were, he reported, thoroughly frightened of the commons. So nervous were they that 'hardly I can cause them to go about to take the leaders of these new commotions'.[1] However, Norfolk's arrival bolstered confidence, and within a few days the first trials and executions had taken place. On 7 February he reached York, and began the task of swearing the gentlemen of the county to the pardon which they had received in December. By the 14th Archbishop Lee had gathered enough confidence to issue a circular to his clergy, denouncing the 'deadly sin' of the original insurrection, and instructing them to preach repentance. At the same time, the commons of Westmorland were 'up' again and were threatening Carlisle, only on this occasion they merely provided a pretext for the gentry to display their loyalty to the Crown, and the rising was dispersed by Sir Christopher Dacre and Thomas Clifford.[2] By the time that the duke arrived with 4,000 Yorkshire horsemen, it was all over. Some 700 of the rebels had been captured, of whom about seventy were dispatched by martial law. The confidence which this success engendered undoubtedly encouraged Norfolk to proceed against some of those involved in the original Pilgrimage, even when there was no evidence of subsequent disaffection. A number of them were sent up to London, including Sir Thomas Tempest, who had been too deeply implicated for his own good. Meanwhile several others, including Aske, Lord Darcy and Sir Thomas Constable, were travelling with the duke, apparently confident that their pardons would hold. They even presented themselves voluntarily at court during March and early April. It may have been suspicion that they had been involved in the abortive rising which had been Sir John Bulmer's response to a similar summons, or it may have been part of Henry's duplicitous purpose from the beginning, but on 7 April the Privy Council wrote to Norfolk to inform him that, owing to the emergence of new evidence, Aske, Darcy and Constable had been committed to the Tower.[3]

In all eighteen people were tried for their involvement in the Pilgrimage and the post-Pilgrimage disturbances. Apart from the three already named, they included Sir Francis Bigod, Lord Hussey, Sir John Bulmer and the former priors of Bridlington and Guisborough. A special commission of oyer and terminer was issued to the Duke of Norfolk and his council on 28 April, and Norfolk then issued a precept to the Sheriff of Yorkshire to empanel a jury on 3 May. As a result the defendants were indicted *in absentia* on 9 May, and the indictments transmitted to London.[4] A parallel commission went through a similar process for Lincolnshire on 12 May. In that case the defendants, Lords Hussey and Darcy, were tried by their peers on the 15th and found guilty. Objectively, as Richard Hoyle has pointed out, the indictments were absurd, alleging conspiracies in places where the defendants had never been, and with people who were not even known to them.[5] However they were not meant to be taken literally, but rather to create a general impression of guilt in support of the evidence presented to the jury. This related almost entirely to the period of the Bigod rising. The council possessed a great quantity of evidence about the October rebellion, but this was not used in the trial, being covered by the December pardon. What was offered was largely circumstantial or consisted of unsupported allegations. It was, for example, urged against Aske that he had concealed his information relating to the January rebellion, and instead of arresting the offenders, had gone about to obtain a pardon for them. Against Darcy it was asserted that he had tried to recover the artillery taken by Aske from Pontefract, although why this should have been thought treasonable is not clear.[6] The most innocent correspondence of January and February 1537 was construed as malicious. The actual trials were a formality and a good example of the way in which Henry used the processes of the law to bring about the convictions which he had already determined upon. In most cases the executions followed swiftly. Bulmer, Tempest and some others were hanged, drawn and quartered at Tyburn on 25 May, and Lady Bulmer was burned at Smithfield on the same day, burning being the prescribed penalty for female traitors.[7] The king could have commuted all these punishments to beheading, but chose not to do so. A further batch, including Bigod, were executed, again at Tyburn, on 2 June, and Lord Darcy, having been formally deprived of the Order of the Garter, was beheaded on Tower Hill on the 30th. A few were taken north, to be executed *in terrorem populi*, Constable at Hull on 6 July, and finally Aske at York on 12 July.[8] Others remained in prison, and one or two died there, but the evidence suggests that Henry regarded the executions as drawing a line under the episode. Norfolk remained in the north until October, but was not called upon to carry out any further investigations. The parliament promised for the north was quietly forgotten. The king obviously felt that Bigod's action had absolved him from all the promises which he had made in December, and it would not have been safe to urge him to the contrary. At first Henry seems to have felt that a progress to the north was called for to capitalise upon his success in dealing with the Pilgrimage, but that was abandoned in June for other reasons. There is no reason to suppose that the north was pacified in any very positive sense, but at least the opposition which remained strong there was sufficiently cowed as to make no further organised protest.

Whether Queen Jane played any part in these proceedings we do not know. If she interceded for any of the victims of Henry's vengeance it has escaped the record, and the chances are that she knew better than to intervene in such a matter. On 16 May Sir Robert Constable wrote to his son, Sir Marmaduke, begging him to get the queen to speak for his life, but it cannot be demonstrated that she ever did so.[9] It would have been sufficient for her to protect her friend Mary from any suspicion of involvement. She can occasionally be glimpsed going about her business. In December 1536, she added her name (and no doubt a handsome donation) to the chantry foundation originally established at Guildford by Eleanor, the queen of King Henry III. In spite of his doubts about the doctrine of purgatory, Henry was quite willing to tolerate this form of piety, and indeed a new foundation had been made in July 1536 by the executors of John Baily at Tamworth in Staffordshire, to pray specifically for the good estate of the king and Queen Jane, as well as for the souls of King Henry VII and Elizabeth his queen, and of the founder and Agnes, his wife.[10] In January 1537 she exchanged presents with Lady Lisle, who also sent a gift to Gertrude, Marchioness of Exeter. Gertrude appears to have been the Chief Lady of the queen's Privy Chamber, and therefore no doubt worth cultivating. In February Jane's sister-in-law, Lady Anne Beauchamp, was delivered of a daughter and on the 22nd she stood godmother at the christening, alongside the Lady Mary. Thomas Cromwell was the godfather, expressing the favour in which he held Viscount Beauchamp at that time.[11] It was always good to be associated with a queen in such good estate as Jane then appeared to be. After some days of uncertainty, toward the end of March the king announced that his wife was pregnant, and he received on the 24th a fulsome letter of congratulation from the Duke of Norfolk, who professed that those around him were rejoicing 'more than anything that I saw'.[12] Whatever doubts Henry may have had about himself were now laid to rest, and all that remained was to pray for a son. His council, upon hearing the news, expressed their relief but pointed out that this now made it imperative for the king to determine the status of his existing daughters in respect of the succession, and to take away 'the remainder hanging upon the King of Scots'. It was to be another six years before he heeded that advice.

News of the queen's pregnancy dominated the small talk of the court that summer. John Hussee could not quite believe it. In writing to Lady Lisle about a present of some dotterels which she had sent to the queen, some of which had died in transit, he reported that Jane 'asked heartily after my lord and your ladyship', and added 'it is said that she is with child. Jesu send her a prince.'[13] In early June came the glad tidings that the queen was 'quickened' with child, that is that she had felt its first movements, and the rejoicings intensified. On 1 June William, Lord Sandys wrote that he had arranged suitable celebrations, including the singing of *Te Deum*s, and the Duke of Norfolk reported that similar festivities were planned for York.[14] Only one thing marred the celebrations, and that was an outbreak of plague. Henry was notoriously jumpy when that infection came anywhere near the court, and Cromwell forbade access to anyone who had been in contact with the disease, but the queen, it would appear, was even more apprehensive. Sir John Russell, writing to Cromwell on 11 July, reported that he had felt bound to tell the king about her extreme nervousness, 'considering that she is with child, and the case she is in', which casts an odd light on the royal couple. Was Henry so unobservant that he had not noticed his wife's fear? Or was she too much in awe of her husband to confide in him? Perhaps Russell was deceiving himself in thinking that the king did not know of his wife's apprehension.[15] Cromwell did not feel bound to do anything about it, so perhaps that is the true explanation. John Hussee obviously had good sources of information within the queen's Privy Chamber, because he picked up the same fear; 'You would not believe,' he wrote to Lady Lisle, 'how much the queen is afraid of the sickness', and yet the mortality in the city was not as great as it had been the previous year, when she had not worried about it at all that we know of. Only 112 people had died of the plague in the week running up to 21 July, so it must have been her pregnancy which made her so fearful.[16] Henry was certainly worried enough about her in other ways, and on 21 June wrote to the Duke of Norfolk putting off his long-anticipated progress to the north until another year. This was a major decision, and was provoked largely by his wife's condition. The council, he declared, had urged him not to go further than 60 miles from her, where he could be recalled if an emergency should arise. What he could have done if such a contingency had arisen is not at all clear, but the council obviously felt that he should remain within reach, perhaps because communications were so slow Meanwhile Chapuys had been withdrawn, and his chatty dispatches cease to be available as sources. His replacement, Diego de Mendoza, arrived in March, instructed to present his credentials to the queen as well as to the king, because one of his objectives was to persuade Henry of the benefits of a marriage between Mary and the infante of Portugal.[17] Jane was obviously thought of as a useful ally in this quest, and one who might even succeed in persuading her husband to restore the princess to her position in the succession. Cromwell did not respond to these suggestions, and instructed Sir Thomas Wyatt, the ambassador with the Emperor, to stall on the proposal until it should appear what the result of the queen's pregnancy should be. 'It is needless to write of the prosperous disposition of the king and queen, which God continue,' he added.[18] During the summer of 1537 Henry was content to remain on good diplomatic terms with the Emperor, but not at all anxious to abandon his friendship with France. It was, after all, their mutual hostility which kept him free from papal interference, as Cardinal Pole's abortive mission had demonstrated.

If Mendoza did present his credentials to the queen, it had no noticeable effect. She had been noted as 'a good Imperialist' at the outset of her marriage, but had been sufficiently warned off political interventions, and had probably contented herself with keeping a 'good disposition' in the king toward his daughter This sufficed to keep the negotiation alive, but not to bring it to any conclusion. As her pregnancy advanced, Jane remained a benevolent presence. On 23 June John Hussee commented on the lacing of her clothes, and she seems to have developed a craving for fat quails, which he was constantly urging Lady Lisle to supply.[19] She did her best, not wishing to forfeit the queen's good opinion, because she was in the midst of a delicate negotiation to persuade Jane to take into her service one of her daughters by her first marriage, either Anne or Katherine Basset. This had been going on since Jane became queen, and the problem seems to have lain not in any inadequacy of the girls but in the absence of a vacancy. However, by the beginning of August the news was better. Thanks to the intercession of the Countess of Sussex, Jane had decided that she would take one of the Basset girls, and on 3 August John Hussee passed on the countess's opinion that they should both present themselves at the court 'before the queen takes her chamber' so that Jane could make a choice.[20] For some reason, Lady Lisle did not immediately respond, and on 1 September Hussee wrote again with a sense of urgency. The queen now desired to see the Basset girls as soon as possible, and they had better appear within a fortnight, because she was due to take her chamber in three weeks, and wished to make a choice before then.[21] Whichever she chose would have a servant to wait on her, and a livery allowance, but only £10 a year by way of a fee. This time the message was received, and on 16 September

Sir Thomas Palmer reported to Lord Lisle that Anne had been the successful candidate, 'and is much commended by everyone'. Katherine was being 'entertained' by John Hussee, and the Lord Privy Seal (Cromwell) had offered his goodwill to them both. On the following day Hussee confirmed the tidings in a letter to Lady Lisle. Anne had been sworn in 'last Saturday' (15 September) 'and furnisheth the room of a yeoman usher', which was perhaps not quite as grand as had been anticipated.[22] Nevertheless the key success had been achieved, and Katherine remained with the Countess of Rutland until Lady Lisle's pleasure was known. She was eventually settled with the Countess of Sussex, and towards the end of the month, Jane 'took her chamber', that is retired for her confinement, at Hampton Court, which suggests that she expected to give birth in late October. Meanwhile she had ordered some changes to Anne's wardrobe, which was apparently too French for her taste. On 2 October John Hussee reported that such changes had been put in hand by Lady Sussex, but that Lady Lisle was expected to supply the extra garments before the queen's churching, which would follow the birth of her child, and was expected to be almost a month away.[23] Henry kept a discreet distance from all this feminine activity. On 3 August, while the plans were still nebulous, it was announced that he would go from Windsor to Grafton on the 8th, where there was expected to be plenty of room for him 'because the queen goes not', and would return to her at Windsor on 2 October. However, by then she had retired to Hampton Court, where he apparently joined her for a few days early in the month. On the 6th Norfolk reported to Cromwell, who was also apparently keeping a safe distance, that because the plague was strong in London, Henry had virtually shut down Hampton Court, apart from the 'queen's proceedings'. He had departed himself, and ordered that no outsiders were to be admitted.[24] One Dr Smythe had already anticipated the worst, because in the middle of August he was denounced for having preached a sermon at St Lawrence's church in Evesham on 8 July in the course of which he had prayed for the king and 'Lady Jane, late queen'. What he thought had happened to her, and what became of him, are alike unknown. At that time she was still being the Lady Bountiful, and on 28 June had ordered the Keeper of Havering Forest to supply two bucks for the gentlemen of the Chapel Royal, probably as a reward for their efforts in celebrating her 'quickening',[25] which had taken place a week or two earlier. Altogether her pregnancy had been normal and easy, and apart from the fear of the plague, kept at bay by Henry's precautions, there must have been considerable optimism in the queen's chamber as the day of her delivery drew near.

Throughout the summer the astrologers had been predicting the birth of a prince. They knew that was what Henry wanted to hear, and they had a 50 per cent chance of being right – or rather better than 50 per cent, considering the number of times that they had been wrong in the past. What they had not predicted, however, was what a struggle the birth would turn out to be. Jane went into labour at some time on 9 October, and when the baby had still not appeared on the 11th, special prayers and intercessory processions were ordered in London. It was reported much later that the child was delivered by Caesarian section, but that cannot have been true, because the operation did not exist at that time.[26] A similar operation was practised, but it inevitably sacrificed the life of the mother and would not have been contemplated in this case. As it was the royal physicians do not seem to have been called upon, and the midwives struggled through two days and three nights to induce the infant to appear. What went wrong we do not know, but it was the small hours of the morning of 12 October before the birth took place, leaving Jane completely exhausted. In the words of the subsequent official announcement,

By the provision of God, Our Lady St Mary and the glorious martyr St George, on the 12 day of October, the feast of St Wilfrid, the vigil of St Edward, which was on the Friday, about two o'clock in the morning, was born at Hampton Court, Edward, son to King Henry VIII...[27]

The child was alive, normal and healthy, and above all it was a boy. At long last God had been good to the king and had blessed him with the heir for which he had striven and manoeuvred for a decade. The cost had been enormous, both in political and in personal terms, but now it all seemed worthwhile. 'God is English', the court preacher Hugh Latimer announced, and the rejoicings were thunderous.

Incontinent after the birth *Te Deum* was sung in Paul's and other churches of the city, and great fires [were made] in every street, and goodly banqueting and triumphant cheer with shooting of guns all day and night, and messengers were sent to all the estates and cities of the realm, to whom were given great gifts...[28]

The same day Jane wrote to Thomas Cromwell, announcing the birth, or someone wrote on her behalf and she signed the letter. He immediately wrote to Sir Thomas Wyatt, instructing him to inform the Emperor of the happy event, and promising a personal letter from Henry. At the same time the King of France was informed by similar means.[29] The news spread with incredible rapidity and by the time that courtly correspondents got around to notifying their country cousins, the latter already knew that England had a prince at last. Henry was understandably gratified. This time the astrologers had got it right, and the stall which he had carefully provided in the Garter Chapel at Windsor Castle would not be wasted.

On Monday 15 October, Edward was christened in the chapel at Hampton Court, the Duke of Norfolk and the Archbishop of Canterbury standing as godfathers, and the Lady Mary as godmother.[30] It was full-blown court ceremony, and no detail was spared to make it impressive. Fear of the plague seems to have been banished, or perhaps it had receded with the advent of cooler weather. All the officers of the household were present, and the procession was led by 'certain gentlemen' bearing unlit torches which were to be ignited at the ceremony itself; there then followed the children and clerks of the chapel royal, led by the dean, and the royal chaplains two by two. After them came such bishops and abbots as were available, and the members of the king's council, followed by the lords, two by two, the ambassadors and the chamberlains. The Lord Privy Seal and the Lord Chancellor then preceded the godfathers, and were followed by the Earl of Sussex and Lord Montague bearing a pair of covered basins to be used in the ceremony. Then came the Earl of Wiltshire 'with a towel about his neck' and bearing the taper of wax which would be lit to signify the child's emergence into the light of the Christian church. The chrisom for the anointing was carried by the Lady Elizabeth, but because of her extreme youth (she was just turned four) she was herself borne in the arms of Viscount Beauchamp, Edward's uncle, in a gesture of extreme confidence.[31] Then at last came the prince himself, carried under a canopy by the Marchioness of Exeter, who was supported in turn by her husband and the Duke of Suffolk. The prince's robe was carried by the Earl of Arundel, and appropriately enough the nurse and the midwife feature at this stage in the procession, kept close to their charge, no doubt, in case of any mishap. Fortunately their services were not required since Edward appears to have slept soundly throughout. The canopy was carried by a select group of gentlemen of the Privy Chamber, including Thomas Seymour, and was followed by the Lady Mary, whose train was borne by Lady Kingston. The ladies of the court then brought up the rear 'in the honour of their degrees'.[32]

When the moment of christening actually arrived, all the torches were lit, and Garter King of Arms proclaimed his name and titles.

Edward was recognised as Duke of Cornwall and Earl of Chester from birth, and these were the titles which were proclaimed, but he was not created Prince of Wales. Although that was the designation of the first-born son of the monarch, it was also by tradition conferred subsequently at a separate ceremony, and it may be that Henry was minded to let him grow a little before bestowing this dignity upon him. In the event Edward was still waiting to be created Prince of Wales when death overtook his father nearly ten years later. At the christening the lords and ladies duly discharged their offices, and when, as was the custom, he proceeded straight to confirmation, the Duke of Suffolk took over as godfather 'to the bishop'. After the completion of this ceremony, the company was given a formal collation of spices, wafers and wine, and the rest of the congregation, who had not formed part of the procession, were given bread and sweet wine. 'The going homeward was like the coming outward, saving that the salt and the basin were left and the gifts of the gossips carried...'[33] These gifts, which had presumably been taken to the chapel in advance, consisted for the most part of pieces of plate, of the same kind as those traditionally given as New Year gifts by the king. The Lady Mary received a cup of gold, the archbishop 'two bowls and two great pots of silver and gilt' and the Duke of Norfolk the same. The Lady Elizabeth 'went with her sister Mary ... to bear the train', this time apparently unassisted, and the trumpets sounded as the company withdrew to the palace. The prince was then borne to his father and mother to receive their blessings, and was solemnly blessed again by the archbishop. After this we are told that the king gave 'a great largesse', which no doubt reflected his triumphant state of mind.

The one person who is virtually absent from this scene of jubilation is Jane. While Henry watched the proceedings from his gallery, she appears to have sat in the antechapel, receiving the gifts and congratulations of her well-wishers. She was weak from her ordeal, and Cromwell later blamed her servants for allowing her to catch cold, but she seems to have been warmly wrapped on this occasion.[34] Nevertheless her health soon began to give cause for alarm. Three days later, perhaps as a result of poor hygiene, she developed puerperal fever, and her life was in danger. Puerperal fever was an infection the transmission of which was poorly understood in the sixteenth century, even by learned medics, and the importance of cleanliness when dealing with the sick was simply ignored. So it is entirely possible that it was not cold which brought about Jane's death, nor the fact that she was given unsuitable things to eat, but simply the failure of her servants to wash either her or themselves adequately after dressing her or attending to her wound.[35] By 23 October she was very ill and had become delirious. On the 24th the Earl of Rutland, who was in touch with the queen's Privy Chamber through his wife, wrote anxiously to Cromwell that the queen had been very sick all the previous night, and that her confessor had administered the last rites. On the same day the Duke of Norfolk, who also had good means of knowing what was going on, also wrote to the Lord Privy Seal that 'for our mistress there is no likelihood of her life' and he feared that she would be dead before his letter came to hand.[36] His fears were justified because Jane died later that same day, which was a Wednesday. The news was not at once believed, and on the Friday, which was the 26th, Sir Thomas Palmer wrote to Lord Lisle to say that there was a rumour that the queen had died on Tuesday, but he knew that she had been alive on the Wednesday, and hoped that the whole report was ill-founded; 'if good prayers can save her, she is not like to die, for never was lady so much [pitied] with every man rich and poor...'[37]

It was a fitting tribute to her gentleness and her popularity, but unfortunately the report was true; Jane was dead, and within a few days of her greatest triumph, the birth of Prince Edward. Henry had not, apparently, been with her at the end. Perhaps her attendants had been anxious to spare him the last moments of a delirious woman, or possibly their menfolk had not wanted to carry the responsibility. After all, Rutland and Norfolk had written to Cromwell when the tidings were desperate, not to the king. However he was informed almost at once, and took the news hard. Not only had he lost the one woman for whom he seems to have felt a genuine affection, but he had lost the precious prospect of further children, and hopefully even a second son to fill up the cup of his happiness. Within a few days the king had written to inform the Emperor and the King of France of his loss, and Cromwell followed these letters up with others of his own, saying that although the king had taken his wife's death with a Christian resignation, he was not disposed to marry again.[38]

Anne Basset, so recently recruited, was now unemployed, and took refuge with the Countess of Sussex until she could secure some fresh appointment, while for those who had not been emotionally involved with Jane, a great deal of tidying up remained to be done. An inventory was prepared of her jewels, which is remarkable mainly for the evidence which it provides of the queen's generosity to those about her. Many of the items are listed as having been given to Lady Mary, Lady Lisle and those numerous ladies of the court with whom she is not known to have had a close association.[39] No doubt gifts also came in but she does not seem to have been much concerned with personal adornment, and unless there was a second inventory which does not survive, she seems to have been abstemious in that direction, unlike Anne, who adored personal finery. A valuation was also drawn up of her lands 'lately parcel of Queen Jane's jointure and dowry and now reserved unto the King's Highness's own hands', showing estates and manors in nine counties, together with the stewards and other officers responsible for their management.[40] Cromwell also prepared a summary of debts owed to the queen, which give some idea of how she conducted her affairs. A sum, for instance, was due from Richard Warren of Beaconsfield, Buckinghamshire 'for money due to Henry Seymour, Receiver of Berkhamstead and King's Langley', which indicates that she had paid Richard's debt to her brother when he was unable to raise the money. If this was true, it gives a good indication of why Jane was so popular. Other money was owed for more routine business transactions, from the farmers of various lands and for a wood sale at Kingsdown in Kent, although how long any of these debts had been outstanding is not apparent.[41]

Queen Jane's body was prepared for burial in the normal way and lay in state for several days at Hampton Court, watched over by her ladies and the other servants of her household. On 28 October her place of interment had not been decided, presumably because Henry could not bring himself to contemplate the prospect, but by 1 November he had decided upon Windsor. Monday 12 November was named as the date, and the Duke of Norfolk and Sir William Paulet began to assemble a suitable cortege.[42] Jane was the first Queen of England to die 'in good estate' since Elizabeth of York in 1503, so there was a good deal of digging around for precedents as to what should happen and who should be in attendance. On 1 November Paulet and Norfolk wrote to Cromwell to say that they had discovered that 'at the interment of Queen Elizabeth were present seven marquises and earls', sixteen barons and sixty knights, in addition to forty esquires and numerous members of the king's household. But they could, they thought, do better than that. Starting with Norfolk himself, they had summoned the Duke of Suffolk, the Marquises of Dorset and Exeter, and the Earls of Surrey, Oxford, Rutland, Wiltshire, Sussex, Hertford and Southampton, the Lord Privy Seal (Cromwell himself) and the Lord Chamberlain (William, Lord Sandys). This, they thought, with a supporting caste of barons and knights, would do sufficient honour to the deceased.[43] According to Richard Gresham, who wrote to Cromwell on 8 November, the duke had ordered on his own initiative 1,200 masses to be sung for Jane's soul, a conservative gesture which she would surely have appreciated. In Gresham's opinion a dirge at St Paul's would also be appropriate, and he asked Cromwell to ascertain the king's pleasure in that respect. Apart from determining the day and place of her burial, Henry seems to have left all the details to his servants, and given the fact that he was punctilious about ceremonies, this seems to have been a fair measure of his distress. We are told that 'of none in the realm was it more heavelier taken than of the king's majesty himself, whose death caused the king immediately to remove into Westminster, where he mourned and kept himself close and secret at great while...'[44] Fortunately, custom forbade him to attend the actual interment, so he was spared a trip to Windsor, but his mourning extended over the Christmas, which was kept with 'small joy' that year. Another person who was deeply distressed was Jane's friend, the Lady Mary. Partly because of that friendship, and partly because of her status as 'second lady', Mary was named as chief mourner; but she was so 'accrased' that she was unable to appear at the first stage of the obsequies, which involved the removal of the body from her chamber to the chapel at Hampton Court on 28 October. By the time that 12 November came, however, she had recovered sufficiently to taker her place in the funeral procession, which moved by easy stages from Hampton Court to Windsor.[45] There, in a vault beneath the Garter Chapel, Queen Jane was laid to rest; she was about twenty-eight years old, and the only one of Henry's queens about whom no one (apart from Martin Luther) had an ill word to say. When his own time came, nearly ten years later, it was beside her that he chose to be laid, instead of near his own parents in Westminster Abbey, which was surely a sign of the special regard in which he held her.

The following day, Bishop Cuthbert Tunstall of Durham informed Cromwell that he had sent a letter of condolence to the king, but that he had not 'dilated the matter too long' lest he 'press too sore upon a green wound'.[46] Similar letters came in from the courts of

Europe, that from the Doge of Venice being dated 24 November. This might have been doubly welcome in that it did not, as did the epistles from the Emperor and the King of France, hint that Henry would now be looking for a new wife. The council shared this concern, but for the time being the king was not interested. He had his son and his memories, and at forty-six years old he was beginning to doubt his capacity to father more children, which was the main point of marriage. Nor did the question of a foreign alliance appear urgent at the end of 1537. The agenda of courtship could wait while he came to terms with his grief.

5

FAMILY POLITICS

Sir Edward Seymour's dispute with Lord Lisle over the reversion of his first wife's estates in Somerset had gone to arbitration in March 1534. Partly because of the legal tangles which were involved and partly because of the influence of rival pressure groups at court, the arbitrators, who included Thomas Cromwell, were in no hurry to produce a decision. Cromwell favoured Lisle, but was obliged to defend himself against accusations of bribery before the council in October 1534. He did manage to obtain a decision in Chancery in Lisle's favour on a related issue, but only because Seymour was willing to accept a part payment instead of the full sum which was due.[1] Eventually in the summer of 1535, the arbitrators came up with a compromise formula, whereby Lisle was bound to mortgage the Somerset estates to Seymour in return for £424. This was duly entered into in April 1536, to run for six months until Michaelmas, and the payment apparently came directly out of Sir Edward's pocket, because although it was negotiated through a London merchant called Holles, Cromwell later spoke of 'this last shifte of iiiic xxiv li ... made with Mr Hollys to his (Seymour's) use', which indicates the true source of the money.[2] He had already loaned Lisle £400 on the security of those same lands in 1532. He had probably been disappointed when that loan had been repaid on time, and in 1536 he set out deliberately to obstruct the perpetually impoverished viscount in his attempts to raise the redemption money. Lisle needed either a loan from the king or a grant of monastic lands, and he found himself frustrated in both quests. In the first place several of his friends in the Privy Chamber, notably Sir Henry Norris and Francis Weston, had disappeared in the trauma surrounding the fall of Anne Boleyn, so he found himself referred to the Court of Augmentations in his quest for a monastic grant. This, as John Hussee observed, 'is very costly for it is new begun and no man knoweth the order thereof but they' (that is the officers), and unfortunately the attorney was one of his creditors, while the Chancellor was a friend of Edward Seymour.[3]

Moreover, his opponent had also undergone a change of fortune. He who had been Sir Edward Seymour, a Groom of the Privy Chamber, was now Viscount Beauchamp and the king's brother-in-law. Jane's marriage to Henry wrought a sea-change in Edward's influence in the Privy Chamber, of which he rapidly became a Gentleman.[4] The autumn of 1536 was also not a good time to trouble the king with requests for favours, as both he and Thomas Cromwell were preoccupied with the Pilgrimage of Grace, and money was in short supply. It was said that credit had never been harder to come by in the City of London than it was in these months, and although the king now had monastic properties to dispense, there were many others who stood in that queue ahead of Lord Lisle. The Chancellor, Richard Rich, simply refused to hear his suit for the parsonage and priory of Frithelstock, Devon on the grounds that there were many more urgent petitions to address. The possession of Frithelstock would have given Lisle the security which he needed to raise a loan in the City, and without it he had no collateral to offer. Moreover Lisle already owed the king money for previous loans which he had failed to repay. According to Sir Brian Tuke, he had not received a penny of Lisle's debts since he took office (in 1528), and though he had blocked a number of Privy Seals and prevented suits against him, he was not prepared to do that indefinitely.⁵ Thanks to Thomas Cromwell, Lord Beauchamp was willing to extend the deadline for repayment from Michaelmas to the end of the year, and then for a further few weeks; but he would not budge beyond that, and foreclosed on the lands. So Lisle needed friends, and Hussee did his best to provide them. First he tried Sir Thomas Henneage, who offered his services in return for eleven dozen fat quails and a hogshead of Gascon wine. In 1537 he approached Sir Thomas Wriothesley, who also proved amenable in return for a bribe of £40.⁶ However these new friends were not the equals of the ones who had been lost, and Hussee quickly became disillusioned with their efforts – or lack of the same. The fact was that they were quite willing to promote Lisle's suits, for a consideration, but not when they discovered that he was opposed by the king's brother-in-law.

Hussee's efforts to find the redemption money during June, July and August 1536 were not entirely without result. He managed to raise a gift of 100 marks from the king, but that was nowhere near enough, and complex negotiations to raise a loan in London eventually came to nothing because of Lisle's inability to offer suitable security.⁷ The failure of the chief putative lender to turn up for a meeting on 15 November sealed the fate of this particular project, and it was more than suspected that Lord Beauchamp had successfully deterred him. Attempts dragged on into 1537, but all were eventually unsuccessful for the same reason. Lisle's position was made more desperate by the fact that the law, or the relevant parts of it, were on Seymour's side. As early as 1533 Leonard Smith, Lisle's attorney, informed Lady Lisle that 'the best for my lord is very naughte'.⁸ However, at that stage Seymour lacked the influence to exploit his advantage, and although he was judged to have handled the situation 'very craftily' was unable to secure his full legal rights. In October 1536 Cromwell wrote to Lord Beauchamp, asking him to put off the day of the redemption of the mortgage, and although he refused he did eventually agree to a delay, possibly after a personal intervention by the king. On 18 November and 5 December he made further concessions, but Christmas came and went without any sign of the money. It was eventually delivered towards the end of January, but Beauchamp refused to receive it, claiming quite rightly that the expiry date was long since past, and that he would enjoy full possession of the Somerset estates. This he apparently did, and the issue disappears from the records.[9] He had been reasonably flexible, thanks to the intervention of Thomas Cromwell and possibly the king, but with the law on his side and his new-found influence in the Privy Chamber, he was not to be baulked on an issue of such importance.

It was within days of his sister's marriage to the king that the extent of the latter's favour to Edward Seymour became clear. On 5 June he was raised to the peerage as Viscount Beauchamp, and within the next month had received a clutch of manors in Wiltshire 'to hold to the said Edward and the heirs male of his body by Lady Anne his wife'. These lands were granted in chief, and no service was specified. Nor was this all; later that same month he was also granted the site and lands of the late priory of Holy Trinity at Eston, also in Wiltshire, and part of the lands of Stanley Abbey in the same county. This grant was similarly made to himself and his heirs male, and no purchase price was mentioned.[10] They must therefore have been gifts from the king, and marks of that especial favour which aimed to make Lord Beauchamp a magnate among his peers, as was appropriate for one who now bore a close blood relationship with the monarch. Chapuys obviously thought of him as a useful ally, and on 6 June, in addition to describing the satisfaction of the people with the king's marriage, went on to relate that he had spoken to the queen's brother,

whom I left very well informed of the great good it would be, not only to the queen his sister, and all their kin but also to the realm and all Christendom likewise if the princess were restored to her rights...[11]

Whether Lord Beauchamp ever raised this delicate subject with the king we do no know, but probably not as this was the time when Henry was particularly exercised about Mary's submission, and few days later the ambassador reported that the king had been very angry with his daughter and had 'rudely rebuffed' Jane's attempts to intercede for her.[12] However, the princess had since submitted to her father, and he hoped that a reconciliation had been affected. Lord Beauchamp must have been in attendance on the king during the autumn of 1536, and as we have seen was summoned with 200 men to go against the northern men on 2 October. This means that he would have been present at the Ampthill Musters, and supported the Duke of Suffolk in Lincolnshire later in that month, although whether he accompanied the Duke of Norfolk to Doncaster in November is not clear. Both he and Jane would have been concerned by their father's declining health, and in December 1536 he died at Wolf Hall. He had not been active on county affairs for some years before his death, and that indicates that his demise was not unexpected. He was in debt to the king when he died, and Margery's jointure would have required some negotiation, but he may have died intestate because it was October 1537, some ten months later, that Lord Beauchamp was eventually given livery of his lands.[13] There is no other explanation for the delay. It was certainly not due to any to any lack of favour. On 27 January 1537 the Duke of Norfolk surrendered the valuable stewardship of Abingdon Abbey in his favour, and it is hard to imagine him doing that without a hefty shove from the king. At the end of March Henry also carried out a characteristic manoeuvre. Having decided that he wanted a house in Kew which belonged to Lord Beauchamp, he offered him in exchange a house in the Strand owned by the Bishop of Coventry and Lichfield. The bishop,

Rowland Lee, was not happy, and demanded of Cromwell what he was to receive in recompense for so convenient a dwelling. Whether he was eventually satisfied or simply browbeaten we do not know, but a month after his original letter, on 3 May, he wrote again, saying that he was willing (of course) to do the king's bidding, but was still uncertain what he was to gain in return.[14] Lord Beauchamp, meanwhile had moved into a house which was much more conveniently placed for the court, which was presumably the motivation behind the whole operation. Henry wanted his brother-in-law near at hand. This was emphasised by the part which Beauchamp played in the proceedings against the 'northern men' in May 1537. He was named to the commission of oyer and terminer for the trial of the commoners, and was a member of the jury of indictment, serving also on the Earl Marshall's court for the trials of Lords Darcy and Hussey, where he returned his 'guilty' verdict along with the rest.[15] He was obviously considered to be a safe pair of hands.

Lord Beauchamp's financial affairs appear sporadically in the records, mostly in connection with his long-running feud with Lord Lisle, which can be largely reconstructed from the correspondence of John Hussee. Lisle's man of affairs, who was frequently driven close to despair by his master's thriftlessness and general incompetence. However, this was not Beauchamp's only entanglement. As a man with interests in many counties he also became involved in a dispute with Lord Dawbeny over lands in Gloucestershire. These were worth £100 a year, but we do not know any details of the dispute, except that at the end of May 1537 the issue was still uncertain at law.[16] Probably Beauchamp used his influence at court to get it resolved in his favour. In August of the same year he was granted a couple of manors in Wiltshire, worth £159 a year, although whether these were a gift or a purchase is not clear. Then in October a valuation was taken of his lands. This was probably done in connection with his elevation to the

Earldom of Hertford, a title which had been vacant since the death of Gilbert de Clare in 1314, and which was bestowed upon him on 18 October.[17] It is natural to suppose that this was connected with the birth of Prince Edward on the 12th, to give the uncle of the new heir to the throne a proper status among the nobility, but it could equally have been the culmination of that favour which had been growing noticeably over the previous year. Henry obviously found Edward Seymour a useful agent and probably an agreeable companion. At that time his lands were valued at £1,107 6s 8d, which was sufficient to maintain the dignity of an earl. Of this £430 was listed as coming of his inheritance, and £604 of the king's gifts. He was also in receipt of an annuity of £13 6s 8d for his creation as Viscount Beauchamp, and of another £20 a year on his elevation to the earldom, sums which should be seen as mere gestures, because his wealth was deemed sufficient in other ways. These, with various other small sums, made up the total listed. Of this total, he was committed to paying his bailiffs and stewards £91 15s, his mother's jointure of £60 a year, and an annuity to one Quynton of £24. He was also by this time committed to paying Lord Lisle an annuity of £120, which presumably marks the final settlement of their long-running dispute, leaving him with a net disposable income of £811 11s 8d.[18] It should be noted that this was not all derived from land; the £20 annuity for his earldom for instance coming from the customs of Southampton. Nor did it apparently include the fees of his various offices, such as the Captaincy of Jersey, and his numerous stewardships. His true income was probably well in excess of £1,000 a year, and an estimate of £1,700 dated 1540 may well be a truer reflection of his prosperity at this earlier date.

The death of Edward's sister the queen does not seem to have diminished him very much, and although he was described in the following year as being 'of small power', that may reflect his unwillingness to do any more for Mary rather than any real diminution of his status.[19] Jane died on 24 October, and while the king retired to mourn in private, he ordered the Duke of Norfolk and Lord Paulet to arrange her obsequies. These were elaborate; first the wax chandler removed her entrails and embalmed the corpse, then the plumber 'leaded, soldered and chested' her, and on the 28th she was removed to the chapel where all the ladies and gentlewomen of her chamber 'put off their rich apparel' and donned mourning attire, kneeling around the body during the mass and the dirge which followed it. Watch was kept in the chapel every night by the gentlemen ushers, and on 1 November the chief mourner, the Lady Mary, appeared for the first time at the offertory. Mass was said every day by a different prelate, until on 12 November the corpse was removed for its interment at Windsor.[20] Starting in the dark, at five o'clock in the morning, it made its way by easy stages, suitably welcomed by clergy and civic dignitaries at each stop, and accompanied by five coaches bearing all the ladies of her chamber and household, some forty-five in number. The cortege was escorted by noblemen, including the Earl of Hertford, and by the officers of arms. It arrived at Windsor soon after 11 o'clock, and the interment was completed by 12 o'clock, when the mourners and other escorts withdrew to the castle for a suitable collation. This was very much a royal occasion, with great emphasis on Jane's status as queen, and her family were not greatly involved. As far as we know, her mother was not even present, and neither of her brothers were given a conspicuous role. Although he was much the more prominent, Edward was not the only Seymour brother around the court at this time. Sir John's third son, Henry, remained firmly anchored at Marriotts in Hertfordshire, and served the king on local commissions, but never aspired to higher things. However the fourth son, Thomas, followed Edward and Jane to the court, and was soon revealed to be an ambitious and talented man.

Born in about 1509, it is not quite clear whether Thomas was older or younger than his sister Jane. Nothing is known of his childhood or upbringing, except what can be deduced from his accomplishments later. He was literate and had a reasonable command of French, but no Latin beyond what was necessary to understand the liturgies of the church, which suggests that he was taught his letters, like his sister and brothers, at home, probably by a chaplain of his father.[21] At some point before 1530 his father placed him in the service of the prominent courtier Sir Francis Bryan. Bryan, however, was also a kinsman, and this arrangement may have been a family one. At what point it commenced we do not know, nor whether Thomas had any position in his own right before his sister caught the king's eye. Given the usual *cursus honorem*, it is probable that he held some relatively humble Privy Chamber position, such as yeoman usher, before he was elevated to the ranks of the Gentlemen on 2 October 1536, but we cannot be sure.[22] Bryan was man of considerable influence, and would have been quite capable of securing such a position for his young protégé, irrespective of Jane. It seems to have been the birth of Prince Edward rather than his sister's marriage which transformed his position, because he was one of the six gentlemen who held the canopy over the prince at his christening on 15 October 1537, and three days later he was knighted at the same ceremony which saw Edward advanced to the dignity of Earl of Hertford.[23] Nor does he appear to have been charged the normal 20 shilling fee for his dubbing. It is possible that these were rewards for earlier services, but the timing does not fit that explanation. In February 1537 Lord Lisle was informed that 'Sir John Dudley goes to the seas with the queen's brother and four of the king's ships'. This brother was certainly Thomas, and Dudley was commissioned as Vice-Admiral.[24] There is no trace of a similar commission being issued to Thomas Seymour, but a fortnight later he turns up as the captain of the *Sweepstake*, one of four ships sent out to curb the activities of Flemish pirates operating in the Channel. On 4 March Sir Thomas Wingfield wrote to John Whalley, 'Tell my cousin Candish that master Seymour, the captain of the *Sweepstake*, thanks him for his cables, else had they died in foul weather', which suggests a rescue operation of some kind.[25] For the next few weeks he joined with Dudley in sending back reports of their patrolling activities, but they seem to have enjoyed little success. Being associated with Dudley in the command of such an operation, as well as being in charge of a royal ship of 300 tons, suggests a measure of experience at sea. We have no means of knowing how that was acquired, but several years of service as a gentleman volunteer would normally have been needed, and it is reasonable to suppose that Thomas had been active aboard the king's ships for several years before we first have notice of him doing so. It would also be consistent with what we know later of his swashbuckling personality. It may well be that his career was independent of that of his sister, because his first significant reward, his appointment as Forester of Enfield Chase, came in August 1532, while Jane was still in attendance upon Catherine of Aragon.[26] In 1537, while she was queen, he received the stewardship of Chirk and Holt castles in Denbighshire, and several manors and lordships in the Welsh Marches. He also received some former monastic lands, but not enough to bring his income anywhere near that of his brother. Wolf Hall, of course, went to Edward when their father died in December 1536, and what Thomas may have inherited remains obscure. We do not even know where he was based when not at court, and it may well be that he rented a house in the London area. It is unlikely that he kept an establishment in any of his Welsh Marcher properties, although he may have done so in one of the Berkshire or Essex properties granted to him in March 1538.[27]

Thomas also remained unmarried, which prompted the Duke of Norfolk to seek a match between him and the duke's widowed daughter the Duchess of Richmond. Mary Howard had endured a few months of unconsummated matrimony with Henry's bastard son the Duke of Richmond, who had died at the age of seventeen in July 1536, and was undoubtedly looking for a satisfactory mate. Just why the duke should have been so keen on Sir Thomas, however, is something of a mystery. He was clearly a personable man, and endowed with the military virtues of courage and boldness, but that can hardly have been a factor, especially as the duchess herself seems to have been opposed to the idea. It was not his wealth, which appears to have been adequate for a Gentleman of the Privy Chamber but no more. Probably the idea arose out of an ambition on the duke's part to establish a marriage link to the royal family, especially as Jane was relatively young and could be expected to have many years ahead of her as queen.[28] However, he persisted with the idea after Jane's premature death, and one can only suppose that he had his eye on Prince Edward's uncle, perhaps with a view to the future of Howard influence when the ageing Henry passed on. Seymour himself appears to have been receptive to the idea, but the Earl of Surrey, Norfolk's son and heir, who was very conscious of his lineage, was bitterly opposed to the prospect of his sister marrying such a base-born fellow as the fourth son of a Wiltshire gentleman and that, combined with Mary's own dislike of the prospect, was sufficient to kill off the negotiation.[29] Surrey is supposed to have suggested to his sister that she might console the king in his widowed state by becoming his mistress, but that outraged her sense of propriety, and she died eventually, unmarried, in 1557. Surrey, like his father, had his eye on the future of Howard influence, and may have had the example of Anne Boleyn in his mind. She had, after all, dangled her charms so seductively before Henry that he had married her. What were the chances of his sister Mary carrying out a similar coup? We do not know what the duke thought of such a scheme, if he ever found out about it, and in any case Mary's unwillingness left it dead in the water.

Jane's brother Henry, as we have seen, remained rooted in local affairs and does not come into this courtly story at all, but her younger sister Elizabeth features briefly and quite prominently. As a young woman she had married Sir Anthony Ughtred, but he had died by 1537, leaving her with at least one daughter, and in straitened circumstances. Acting probably on Jane's advice, in June of that year she wrote to Thomas Cromwell, reminding him that when she was last at court he had offered to help her if she was ever in need. That time had now come. 'In Master Ughtred's days,' she went on, 'I was in a poor house of mine own, but since then I have been driven to be a sojourner, for my living is not sufficient to entertain my friends...'[30]

This profession of dependence should, however, be treated with a certain scepticism, as Sir Arthur Darcy was writing to her at about the same time as though she controlled access to the royal bounty herself. He wanted the parsonage of Asskrygg in Yorkshire, which had belonged to the Abbot of Jervaulx, 'for forty years at the old rent'. 'If she speaks but a word to the king she may have it, and he will give her £100 for it.'[31] It may be that word had already reached him of the manner in which Cromwell was proposing to solve Elizabeth's problems, for he spoke darkly of 'some southern lord' causing her to forget the north, and of rumours that she should 'have her train borne at Hennyngham', which seem to be allusions to a forthcoming wedding. By the middle of the following month it was generally known that 'my Lord Privy Seal's son and heir shall shortly marry my Lady Ughtred, Lord Beauchamp's sister', and by 3 August the nuptials were completed.[32] The Duke of Norfolk was not the only man to be seeking a matrimonial alliance with the royal family, but Cromwell was clearly in a better position to bring his schemes to effect. It is not known that Lady Ughtred raised any objections to what was for her a timely rescue, and in a chatty letter to Cromwell towards the end of August Edward, Lord Beauchamp sent commendations to his sister and brother-in-law; 'and I pray God shortly send them a nephew'.[33] This last wish was not granted for some time, as when Thomas's

Jane Seymour by Hans Holbein. She was not a great beauty, but carried little political baggage, and
d no agenda of her own. She was greatly praised for her sweet disposition.

Above: 3. St Mary's church, Great Bedwyn, where many members of the Seymour family are buried. *Opposite*: 6. Sir Thomas Seymour, Lord Seymour of Sudeley, from a stained glass window at Sudeley Castle. Thomas was Jane's brother, and after Henry VIII's death married his widow, Catherine Parr, who he had been pursuing before her marriage to the king.

Above: 4. Funeral effigy of Sir John Seymour, Jane's father, from St Mary's church, Great Bedwyn. *Right*: 5. Memorial brass to John Seymour, Jane's elder brother, who died before 1520. Nothing is known about his short life.

Above: 7. Jane's second brother, Edward Seymour, Duke of Somerset and Lord Protector of England (1547-9). He was also appointed Governor of the King's Person to Edward VI, Jane's son by Henry, in consideration of his close blood relationship. *Right*: 8. Jane's badge of the phoenix, coupled with the Tudor rose, from a stained glass window at St Mary's church, Great Bedwyn.

Left: 9. Jane, from a group portrait of Henry VIII and his family, designed to emphasise the importance of Prince Edward as the king's heir. *Opposite*: 10. Prince Edward, Jane's son by Henry VIII (later King Edward VI) as an infant, by Hans Holbein. Edward was born on the 12 October 1537, and this drawing was made at some time before Holbein's death in 1543.

Top left: 12. Anne of Cleves. Henry's marriage to her following Jane's death was a mistake born of his need for a German ally. Their marriage lasted less than six months. *Above left & Above right:* 13. & 14. Henry VIII. The iconic portrait by Hans Holbein, showing the king as he wished his subjects to perceive him. Henry VIII in later life, when the effects of hard living were beginning to show. An unflattering portrait from a boxwood carving at Sudeley Castle.

Opposite: 11. Anne Boleyn, the wife whom Jane displaced. Her feisty sexuality left her vulnerable to political attack by those she had offended in the course of her rise to power. *Above:* 15. Catherine Parr, Henry's sixth and last queen, who subsequently married Lord Thomas Seymour. Jane's son Edward's education was overseen by Catherine. From a funeral effigy at Sudeley, where she died in September 1548.

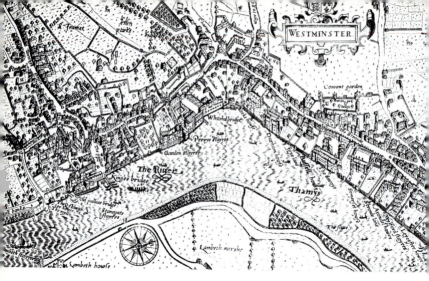

Above: 16. John Norden's plan of Westminster (1593). This near contemporary plan shows Westminster as Jane would have known it. The palace was the centre of government, and was surrounded by other palaces and homes belonging to nobles, courtiers and royal servants. The City was close enough to London for the two to be seen as a single unit. *Below*: 17. The Coronation procession of Jane's son Edward VI in February 1547, passing Cheapside Cross on its way to Westminster Abbey. The windows and rooftops are crowded with spectators, suggesting the enthusiasm of the citizens for their new king.

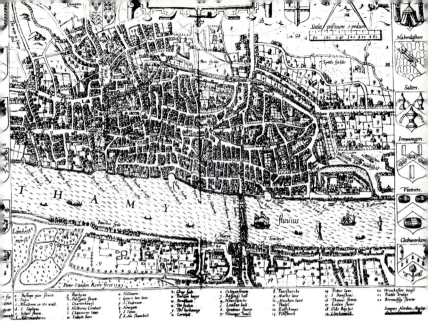

Above: 18. John Norden's plan of London (1593) showing the city from St Katherine's-by-the-Tower in the east to the Temple in the west. Southwark, or Bridge Ward Without is depicted across the river. The suburbs to the north of the City had expanded since the 1530s. *Below*: 19. A distant view of Greenwich Palace, from a drawing by Anthony van Wyngaerde of about 1550, in the Ashmolean Museum at Oxford. Henry installed Jane's brother Edward and his wife in a suite here in March 1536, a sign of the growing favour of the Seymours.

Above: 20. A view of London Bridge and the Tower of London in 1616, by Claes Visscher. The large number of ships in the Pool of London is to be noted. Jane's brother Thomas would later be executed here. *Below*: 21. The White Tower of the Tower of London. The Tower was a palace and fortress as well as a prison, and monarchs traditionally passed the night before their Coronations here. Jane, however, would not have done this; she was never crowned.

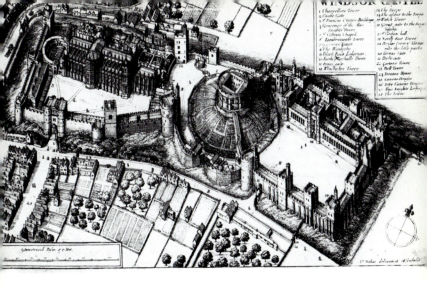

Above: 22. Windsor Castle, where Henry VIII and Jane are buried side by side in a vault below St George's chapel. *Below*: 23. A external view of the queen's apartments at Hampton Court. Anne Boleyn was executed before the work was completed, so her successor Jane was the first occupant.

Above: 24. Oatlands Palace in Surrey. Expanded by Henry VIII from a hunting lodge into a grand residence for Henry's next wife, Anne of Cleves, it was demolished in the seventeenth century. *Left*: 25. Richmond Palace. A favourite residence of Henry VII, the use of it was granted to Cardinal Wolsey in 1525 in return for his gift to the king of Hampton Court. *Below*: 26. Nonsuch Palace. Allegedly modelled on Chambord, it was built by Henry VIII and left incomplete on his death. It was more compact than the great palaces such as Hampton Court, and could not house the whole court. It was thus to some extent a place of retreat.

Above left: 27. Henry VIII in Council. This must have been a special session, when the king had some crucial information to impart, because he did not attend normal Council meetings. *Above right*: 28. The title page of Henry VIII's Great Bible of 1539. This was a propaganda exercise in which the king, as Supreme Head of the Church, is handing the word of God to the laity and the clergy of his kingdom.

29. A nineteenth-century painting, imagining the moment when Cardinal Wolsey learns that the king has dismissed him as Lord Chancellor. Wolsey lost his chancellorship for his failure to rid Henry of Catherine of Aragon so that he could marry Anne Boleyn, and Cromwell would lose his head for his handling of Henry's betrothal to Anne of Cleves. Jane Seymour, however, required no such machinations for her success; she merely caught the eye of the king. The fashionably dressed figure on the right is intended to represent the Duke of Norfolk.

Above left: 30. From the title page of the Great Bible. Archbishop Thomas Cranmer receives the Word on behalf of the clergy. On the day Anne Boleyn died, Cranmer granted Henry a dispensation to marry Jane Seymour despite their consanguinity. *Above right*: 31. From the title page of the Great Bible. Thomas Cromwell, Viceregent in Spirituals, receives the Word on behalf of the laity. After Jane's death, Cromwell would push his king to marry again; the subsequent marriage would result in his execution.

Above left: 32. The Princess Elizabeth, from the family portrait of Henry VIII. No one expected her to succeed to the throne at that time, but the death of Jane's son Edward, at just fifteen, followed by that of Mary five years later, resulted in her forty-four-year reign. *Above right*: 33. Henry Fitzroy, Duke of Somerset and Richmond, the king's illegitimate son by Bessie Blount, who was born on 15 June 1519. His importance to the king at that time was as a proof that he was capable of fathering sons after so many unsuccessful attempts with his wife, Catherine of Aragon.

Above left: 34. Stephen Gardiner, Bishop of Winchester, a diplomat and member of the king's inner circle of advisers. He was the arch rival of Thomas Cromwell, and was mainly responsible for his fall in June 1540. Gardiner would be excluded from involvement in the accession of Jane's son, Edward VI, as Henry considered him too powerful. *Above right*: 35. Princess Mary, from the family portrait of Henry VIII. All the attention was focussed on Prince Edward at that time, and her accession was not anticipated. Mary was only persuaded to submit to the Royal Supremacy at Jane's urging. *Right*: 36. Thomas Howard, 3rd Duke of Norfolk. The Lord Treasurer, and uncle to Queens Anne Boleyn and Catherine Howard, he was a leading councillor and rival to Thomas Cromwell. Having survived the fall of both his nieces, he was convicted of high treason in January 1547, and saved from execution by the death of Henry VIII on the 28th of the month. The fortunes of the Howards often rose at the Seymours' expense, and vice versa.

Ladies' fashions at the court of Henry VIII.
Above left: 37. A lady of the court. Her loose hair indicates that she was unmarried.
Above right: 38. Lady of the court, thought to be Madge Shelton. She is wearing the French-style
bonnet, fashionable during Anne Bolyen's reign. By Hans Holbein. *Below left*: 39. Lady of the
court, dressed in the full version of the French style. By Hans Holbein. *Below right*: 40. Mary
Howard, Duchess of Richmond, and widow of Henry Fitzroy, Henry VIII's only other son, though
illegitimate. A sketch by Hans Holbein.

son, Gregory Cromwell died in 1552 he left his own son Henry as a minor, prompting another begging letter from Elizabeth, this time addressed to Sir William Cecil. Elizabeth rode in the fourth carriage to Jane's interment in November 1537.[34]

Mary, as we have seen, was the chief mourner at these obsequies, and had been very much in her father's mind since their reconciliation in the previous summer. Throughout the summer of 1537 he had been juggling with the related questions of her marriage and status, balancing the infante of Portugal against the Duke of Angoulême, and coming eventually to the conclusion that any marriage would have to be subject to a treaty which would need to be confirmed by parliament.[35] This satisfied neither the French nor the Emperor, because a statute could be repealed and, by leaving Mary no place in the succession, would leave her husband with no prospects in England. No marriage resulted, and there are signs that the twenty-one-year-old princess was becoming increasingly frustrated. Jane's untimely death left Mary as the first lady of the court, and she presided with her father over the ceremonies of the next two years, but there is little sign that she derived much satisfaction from that eminence. Indeed the Christmas of 1537 was spent in mourning for the dead queen, so there was very little chance for her to shine. Apart from her appearances at court, Mary's routine during these years is hard to reconstruct. Her Privy Purse expenses survive from December 1536, but although these provide a lot of circumstantial detail, they do not tell us much about her household, because she was not paying the bills.[36] In theory her establishment remained a joint one with Elizabeth, as it had been during her years at Hunsdon, but of course their respective circumstances had changed completely. Then Elizabeth had been the lawful princess and Mary the bastard daughter; now they were both equally illegitimate and Mary, as the elder, took precedence. She also enjoyed a good deal of freedom of movement. While Elizabeth stayed mainly at Hunsdon, Mary went to Hatfield and Newhall in January 1537, to Westminster in February and to Chelmsford before Easter. Most of the early summer she spent at Greenwich, but during July and August visited Hampton Court, Guildford and Windsor. During Jane's lying-in in October she appears to have been mainly at Richmond, although she may have visited Hampton Court when it was clear that Jane was dangerously ill.[37] In all these migrations she was accompanied by the ladies of her Privy Chamber, but whether she was also attended by part of the menial staff of the joint household remains a matter of speculation, because they were separately paid.

The king's warrant to Sir Brian Tuke, his Treasurer of the Chamber, dated 28 August 1536 sets out what should have happened:

> We will and command you that you incontinent upon the sight hereof do of our money which shall come into your keeping, pay or cause to be paid unto our trusty and well beloved servant Sir John Shelton, knight, steward of the household of our children, the sum of four thousand pounds in advancement of the charges of the said household for one whole year...[38]

Tuke complained that he did not have the money, but his protest was apparently ignored. At the same time the expenses of Mary's Privy Chamber were met by Sir Thomas Henneage, the Chief Gentleman of the King's Chamber, out of the Privy Purse which he held. This money came in dribs and drabs, £40 (about £1,200 in present day money) here, and £20 (£600) there, to meet immediate needs and was controlled by Mary herself. Some £430 (£12,900) was received from this source between December 1536 and December 1537, and disbursed mainly in liveries and in rewards to servants, particularly those who brought small gifts to the princess, which was a frequent occurrence.[39] When she stayed at court, rewards were given to the members of the service departments, such as the cooks of the royal kitchen or the servants of the scullery. No such rewards were given during her other migrations, presumably because they were paid by Shelton off the household account. Mary clearly enjoyed the freedom which these arrangements gave her, and the council's recommendation that both she and Elizabeth be allocated 'some certain decent living' to augment their status and make them more acceptable as royal brides, passed her by completely.[40] Henry did not accept the advice, preferring to retain control, but that seems to have made no difference to his relations with his daughter. While Jane's pregnancy was advancing, Mary seems to have enjoyed herself. She retained a band of minstrels, and her jester 'Jane the Fool' appears for the first time during these months. Her health also appears to have been good, better at any rate than during her years of confinement, and there is only a single reference to her being sick in June 1537.[41] She retained the services of Miguel de la Soa, a Spaniard formerly in her mother's household, as her physician for a fee of 100 marks a year, but he was seldom called upon during this period, and clearly did not 'live in'. He was sent for when need required, but this was usually to attend one of the resident servants rather than Mary herself. The change in her circumstances seems to have brought about a remarkable transformation in her general well-being. There are also suggestions that Mary's service was attractive, particularly to girls whose families were of a conservative turn of mind. Lady Lisle, for instance, tried to place her daughter Kate Bassett with the princess after Anne had been preferred to her in the queen's Privy Chamber. She was not successful because Mary's chamber was deemed to be full in October 1537, but that probably indicates that she was not entirely a free agent, even in the selection of her own ladies.[42] Years later Jane Dormer remembered that it was at about this time that Mary began to acquire a reputation for employing young girls whose families wanted them to be brought up in piety and virtue.

Mary was, however, discreet, and managed to avoid political controversies. It may be for that reason that she failed to acquire a following, except possibly among those families which were seeking to place their daughters. She received no dedications, and indeed seems to have been of no political significance whatsoever. This undoubtedly helped her to stay on good terms with Thomas Cromwell, of whose evangelical agenda she cannot possibly have approved. Having earned her gratitude for his role in securing her reconciliation with her father, he seems to have been determined to keep her in the same frame of mind. He rewarded her servants, sent her small gifts and the occasional word of fatherly advice, and her notes to him were always ones of thanks for such attentions.[43] Although she was now on good terms with her father, he was unpredictable, and she never knew when she might need the Lord Privy Seal's intercession again. Like most of the other courtiers, she was in a sense his client, although he was too sensible to emphasise that fact. When he fell from favour in 1540, she is not known to have moved in any way to his defence. Perhaps she knew her father too well, or perhaps the fact that he was charged with heresy caused her to reappraise their relationship.

The birth of Edward in October 1537 changed her position completely. No loyal Englishman who recognised the legitimacy of Henry's marriage to Jane could now regard Mary as the heir, no matter whether she was legitimate or not. It was of course quite possible to regard them both as legitimate, because Catherine was dead before that marriage took place. Henry toyed with this idea himself, using the argument of *bona fide parentum*, that is that she was legitimate because her parents had entered into matrimony in good faith, the obstacles not then being realised.[44] However he had given up on this explanation before Edward's birth, realising that it constituted a threat to his ecclesiastical supremacy. He therefore continued to insist on Mary's bastardy in any public negotiation relating to her, although he did not rule her out of the succession, after Edward, of course. It was this proviso which kept her in the marriage market, although not really accepted by either the Emperor or the King of France. To Charles, and indeed to the whole of Catholic Europe, she was Henry's only legitimate child. Elizabeth was obviously a bastard, having been born to 'the concubine' while Catherine was still alive; and it was dubious whether she was Henry's daughter at all, given that her mother had subsequently been convicted of adultery. But Edward was equally illegitimate, because Jane had married the king while the realm was in schism, and no lawful matrimony could be contracted. So Mary was illegitimate by the laws of England, Edward by the canon law of the Western Church, and Elizabeth by both. This was a tangle which could not be resolved by any agreed form of litigation, and Henry eventually cut the Gordian Knot by Act of Parliament in 1543.[45] This not only included all three children in the order of succession, but empowered the king to change that order by his Last Will and Testament – an act of sovereignty without parallel. So while Jane rested in her grave at Windsor, her legacy, in the form of a disputed succession, went on for the remainder of Henry's life – and indeed beyond.

6

THE KING'S OPTIONS

So Queen Jane was gone, but she was not forgotten. According to John Smythe (her surveyor), all her tenants in Hampshire, Dorset, Somerset and Wiltshire were 'as glad of her grace' as heart could wish, and deeply mourned her passing.[1] A 'lamentacion' was published in 1560, and Paul Hentzer was shown her bed as a kind of tourist attraction at Hampton Court as late as 1598. In 1575 Ulpian Fulwell published a 'ballad in commemoration of Queen Jane' in his *Flower of Fame*:

Among the rest whose worthy lives
Hath run a virtuous race
O noble fame pause the time,
And give Queen Jane a place.
A nymph of chaste Diana's train,
A virtuous virgin eke,
In a tender gentle matron's heart,
With modest mind and meek...
Whose godly life and final end
I would each lady view
That fame may in her register
For aye her name renew...[2]

King Henry, as we have seen, mourned her deeply, but she also seems to have secured, in her brief reign as queen, a place in the affections of ordinary people. She was Mary's friend, and insofar as she had a political agenda, it was one of peace and reconciliation. She must have seemed the perfect foil for her masterful and capricious spouse, and could be loved by those loyal hearts which could find only respect and fear for the king. In notifying the French of the queen's death at the end of October, Cromwell had been careful to point out that Henry was not disposed to marry again, but he was expressing the king's personal as opposed to his political will.[3] Royal marriages were not about romantic love, and the death of a consort in childbed was an occupational hazard; so within days his council had persuaded Henry that, although he might not feel inclined to it, it was his duty to marry again. His son was a blessing, but more legitimate royal children were an urgent requirement. Both his brother and his own illegitimate son had died young, and the risk of Edward doing the same could not be ignored. A Duke of York was much needed, and the only way to that end was by the king marrying again.[4] There was also the question of a foreign alliance. It was all very well finding a bride within the realm, but a consort's kindred inevitably sought promotions and power. That was only a minor problem as far as the Seymours were concerned, but it had been a major factor with the Boleyns, and not one which the council was anxious to repeat. Thomas Cromwell did not want another Earl of Wiltshire bidding for the king's confidence. He therefore, with the support of his fellow councillors, quickly persuaded Henry to look abroad for a new consort. Within days of Jane's death the English ambassadors in France and the Low Countries were instructed to begin making enquiries.[5] France and the Empire seemed to be close to an agreement to end their perpetual hostilities, and if that happened, England would be seriously isolated, so that a matrimonial alliance seemed one way out of the difficulty. Neither party might be willing to accept the terms which he was prepared to offer, but at least the existence of negotiations would preserve their antagonism for a little longer, or even sabotage their peace proposals entirely.

Although he had recently been seeking improved relations with the Empire, it was nevertheless to France that Henry first looked, and two possibilities were mentioned almost at once. The first was Francis' daughter, Marguerite de France, then aged about fifteen and the second was Marie, the widowed daughter of the Duke of Guise. The latter's praises had been sung loudly by the English ambassador, Sir John Wallop, and she was the favourite.[6] As early as December 1537 Peter Mewtas, a gentleman of the Privy Chamber was sent to sound her out, and returned full of enthusiasm. Henry apparently became quite animated, but he was doomed to disappointment, because by the time that Mewtas returned to France with an offer in February 1538, she was committed to James V of Scotland. Not only was this an unwelcome reminder of the Auld Alliance, it was also an affront to Henry's regal dignity. How could any woman prefer a 'beggerly fellow' like the King of Scots to His Majesty of England?[7] Marguerite may have been thought too young or Francis may have expressed disapproval, but no negotiation for her hand then ensued. Instead Henry turned to the other camp, and began to cast an eye over Christina, the widowed Duchess of Milan. Christina was the daughter of Christian II of Denmark, who had been deposed by his nobles in 1523. This had not apparently reduced her value on the marriage market, and she had been matched with the Duke of Milan in 1535, at the age of thirteen. Widowed within year, she was now sixteen, and had the additional advantage of being a niece of the Holy Roman Emperor, her mother being Charles's sister.[8] By January 1538, before he was rebuffed over Marie of Guise, Henry had become interested in her. She had recently arrived at the court of Mary of Hungary, the Regent of the Low Countries and had attracted a fulsome report from the English ambassador in Brussels, who as we have seen, had been briefed to keep a lookout for possibilities. Henry consequently instructed his ambassador with the Emperor to raise the possibility as though it were his own idea, the plan being to tempt Charles into making an offer.[9]

Had he done so, that would have given Henry the initiative to make demands in return for his consent, but he did not, leaving the king to make all the running. First it was necessary to know what the girl looked like, because Henry was not disposed to trust the second-hand reports which were all he had to go on so far, so before the end of January he dispatched Philip Hoby, another member of his Privy Chamber, with secret instructions to interview her and report back. With Hoby went Hans Holbein, his court painter, who was to bring back a drawing. This mission was successful, Henry was delighted, and it was from the resulting drawing that the celebrated portrait of Christina was painted.[10] The king now felt able to enter into a negotiation for the lady's hand, and was apparently 'merry', talking of nothing but music and pageants. Less than four months after her death, Jane appears to have been forgotten, but Henry was subject to mood changes and periodic bouts of melancholy returned when he thought of her in the midst of his new preoccupations. Marriage was at the heart of his foreign policy at this time; with the Emperor he was discussing his own union with the duchess and a revived plan to marry Mary to Dom Luis of Portugal, and at the same time he was talking to the French ambassador about the possibility of his marriage to Marie of Guise, who was not yet known to be out of the running. There was hypothetical talk of Elizabeth (aged five) and Edward (just a few months) wedding the King of Hungary's son and the Emperor's daughter respectively. It was all highly speculative, and designed above all to protect England from diplomatic isolation.[11] As might be expected, the negotiations were complex and eventually inconclusive. Henry wanted Charles to include him in any future peace treaty with France, and to refuse his support to the General Council of the Church which had been called to Mantua, which the king suspected would be used against him. The Emperor was not prepared to compromise himself in such a fashion, his relations with the papacy were too important. There were also the usual arguments about dowries and rights of inheritance, complicated in this case by the fact that Mary was illegitimate by English law, and the king was prepared to offer no hope of her legitimation. The crown matrimonial of England was not on offer, even as a distant prospect. Then there was the issue of consanguinity involving the duchess, because she was Catherine of Aragon's great niece, and a dispensation was therefore necessary, but who should issue it? The Emperor suggested the Pope, which was unacceptable to the English, and the English offered the Archbishop of Canterbury, who was equally unacceptable to the Habsburgs.[12]

Finally, there was the lady herself to consider. She had reached the canonical age of consent, and could not be treated as a child. Unfortunately she was reported to be far from keen on the prospect of becoming Henry's fourth bride. 'For her council suspecteth that her great aunt was poisoned, that the second was put to death, and the third lost for lack of keeping in her childbed...'

These rumours were less than fair to Henry, but they represented the prevailing opinion in Europe,[13] and Christina appears to have believed them. She therefore withheld her consent, and that eventually proved fatal to the whole negotiation, especially as Mary's prospects were marred by her bastardy. There was nothing left to discuss. While the negotiations were still in progress, however, the French came up with proposals which reconciled Henry to their failure, and shifted the whole emphasis of the discussions. In May 1538 the ambassador suggested that the king might like to consider a match between Mary and Francis' younger son, Charles, while he himself took Louise, Marie of Guise's sister. The king's response was immediate and reflects his anxiety about the collapse of the Habsburg talks. The very next day Sir John Russell was sent to the ambassador with keen enquiries about Louise and a request for a portrait of her.[14] Marillac was also showered with gifts, from a stag to 'great artichokes' from the royal gardens. When the portrait did not arrive promptly, Henry sent Hoby and Holbein on another mission, and in early June they returned with two drawings of the lady, whom they had encountered at Le Havre. Events then began to move rapidly, and do indeed seem to indicate that Jane had been consigned to the past. In the first place the king heard of another French girl, Renee, the sister of Marie and Louise, who was reputed to be even more beautiful than her sisters; then there was Marie of Vendome, Anne of Lorraine, and Francis' own sister Marguerite. In August 1538 Hoby and Holbein were sent on another mission to secure portraits of as many of these ladies as possible, and came back with a good likeness of Anne of Lorraine.[15] By that time, with his suit for Christina still not finally dead, Henry was busily negotiating a match for Mary with Charles de Valois, and one for himself with any one of five French beauties, of three of whom he had likenesses. He was in danger, however, of overplaying his hand, because he had already stipulated that he should be included in any Franco–Imperial treaty, and that Francis should obstruct the papal council. The King of France was not as unwilling as the Emperor had been to meet these conditions, particularly over the council, but still observed that Henry's idea of a bargain was somewhat one-sided. Henry nevertheless persisted, and this casts some doubt on his whole sincerity in these marriage negotiations. He requested that all the French candidates for his hand should be marshalled at Calais so that he could make his choice. The French were astounded by his impudence. Was this kind of cattle sale the way in which the knights of the Round Table treated their womenfolk, the ambassador asked?[16] And Francis was offended. He would send one lady to Calais to be inspected, but that was all.

These negotiations rumbled on into the autumn, but the main objective was lost in June, when Charles and Francis met at Nice under the Pope's mediation and signed a ten-year truce which ignored England altogether. Henry was alarmed. Not only did he face the prospect of censure from a papally inspired council (to which he had, of course, appealed in 1533), but also the possibility that Catholic Europe would now unite against him. He had failed in his diplomatic attempt to exploit Charles's desire for a Habsburg marriage with Mary to extract Milan from the Emperor and thereby provoke Francis into continuing the war, and faced the papacy in the winter of 1538–9 with no political support at all. On 17 December Paul III took another step towards promulgating his Bull of three years earlier deposing Henry and absolving his subjects from their allegiance.[17] What effect this might have had, had the process been completed, we do not know, but Henry was sufficiently alarmed to order the mobilisation of his forces. Two days after Christmas, Cardinal Reginald Pole, who had carried out a similar mission in 1536, set out from Rome to mobilise the Catholic powers against the schismatic king. At the same time David Beaton was made a cardinal and sent home to Scotland to galvanise James V into similar activity. On 12 January 1539 Francis and Charles concluded the formal Treaty of Toledo, each agreeing not to enter into any agreement with England without the other's consent, which appeared to signal at least a breaking-off of diplomatic relations.[18] There were rumours that the ambassadors were about to be withdrawn, and it seemed that a crisis had been reached. In addition to mustering the counties, Henry used some of the proceeds of the Dissolution of the Monasteries to improve the defences of Calais and Guisnes, and to erect a series of forts along the South Coast from Pendennis to Ramsgate.[19] The fleet was mobilised and foreign ships were forbidden to leave English ports. Some of them were requisitioned for royal service, and alarming reports spoke of a hostile navy assembling at Antwerp.

An army was also supposed to be gathering in the Low Countries. Meanwhile, nothing had actually happened. The ambassadors remained in place, and Edmund Bonner and Sir Thomas Wyatt were instructed to do all in their power to prise this unnatural alliance apart, as well as sabotaging the mission of Cardinal Pole, who in May had arrived in Spain on the first leg of his tour.[20]

Still nothing happened. There was no rebellion in England because if there was one thing designed to unite Englishmen behind their king, it was the prospect of foreign intervention against him. Moreover Pole's mission soon ran into the sand without any help from English diplomacy. He might pretend to the French that he found Charles amenable to the idea of an attack, but in fact the Emperor was quite unwilling to add to his enemies; the Turks and the Lutherans were giving him quite enough problems without that. He therefore confined himself to making sympathetic noises, and Pole was so disheartened by his interview that he put off his visit to Francis, sending two emissaries instead. These were informed that while the King of France was perfectly willing to do his duty and attack Henry, he would only do so when the Emperor was prepared to act in concert. He probably knew that Charles had no such intention.[21] He also expressed the view that it would be inadvisable for Pole to come to France at that juncture, lest it arouse suspicion in England and give Henry time to prepare himself. His real intention had already been made clear in a letter to the King of England in early April in which he explained that the warlike preparations which the latter had observed were aimed against the Emperor and not against himself. In other words the Treaty of Toledo was about to break down, to Henry's huge relief.[22] By July he was sufficiently confident to call off his preparations against invasion, which had caused the South East of England to resemble a war zone, with every strategic point being defended by ditches, palisades and ramparts. In August Pole was recalled to Rome, his second mission having proved no more fruitful than his first. The Council of Mantua was postponed *sine die*, and the sentence of excommunication remained unpromulgated. Henry had survived another crisis.[23]

Meanwhile he continued to pursue his own eccentric religious policy. The conservative Act of Six Articles was passed in May 1539, which would surely have delighted Jane, and seems to have gone down well with her brothers. However the Dissolution of the Monasteries continued as the major houses surrendered one by one and their property passed under the control of the Court of Augmentations. In January, while the threat from the Continent still seemed to be acute, he also offered to join the Lutheran League of Schmalkalden. This approach must have been inspired by his urgent need for friends, but was nevertheless cast in the form of a mission to the Duke of Saxony and the Landgrave of Hesse, offering full allegiance to the League.[24] He followed this up in March with a second mission to the King of Denmark and the city of Wismar, both Lutheran powers, proposing an English alliance against the 'papists'. This latter mission probably explains the purposes of both, but Henry may have been considering religious concessions to the Lutherans or at least the appearance of such in order to secure membership of the League, of which he would have become the patron and, in a sense, the leader. The Lutherans responded very coolly to these advances, Christian III of Denmark professing himself unable to send ambassadors to England at that moment, but nevertheless leaving the door open for future negotiations. The League responded similarly. They were unwilling to send a delegation because of the failure of past efforts to reach agreement, and although they did eventually relent, the ambassadors whom they sent were undistinguished.[25] They arrived on 23 April and walked straight into the furore over the Act of Six Articles, which went to the parliament a few days later and which contained provisions which were totally unacceptable to them. When Henry heard that the Lutheran princes at the Diet of Augsburg had come to terms with the Emperor, which the king regarded as an act of betrayal, he told the delegates that they were wasting their time and had better go home. This débâcle was of course connected with the news that the Emperor and the King of France were squaring up for another round of confrontation, and that Henry's need for allies was therefore less urgent than it had been at the beginning of the year. Although the Act of Six Articles had not helped, it was not due to any conservative drift in Henry's religious policy either. That shift was more apparent than real, because the core of Henricianism, the Royal Supremacy, remained untouched, but it did indicate that there was no future in a diplomatic alliance with the League, which regarded adherence to the Confession of Augsburg as a basic requirement.[26] By June of 1539 the king therefore appeared to be running out of options. His approach to the League of Schmalkalden had collapsed, largely through his own inflexibility, and his matrimonial pursuit of the Duchess of Milan and of numerous French ladies had come to nothing. These negotiations had done nothing to prise Charles and Francis apart, but fortunately they had fallen out for reasons of their own which owed nothing to Henry or his schemes.

The king, however, was still in need of a wife, and time was not on his side. He was now forty-eight, corpulent and not in the best of health. If he did not get on with the business of begetting more children, it would be too late. So he began to look for a lady who was neither Imperialist nor French, nor Lutheran, and remarkably, such a one was available. An alliance with the Duke of Cleves had been mooted as early as June 1538, but at that time had been buried beneath the pile of other negotiations which were then going on. Duke John of Cleves was not a prince of first-class power, but he was at loggerheads with the Emperor over his inheritance of the County of Gelderland, which had taken place in July 1538. He was not a Lutheran, but might be described as an Erasmian humanist, and his relations with the papacy were almost as bad as

Henry's own. Moreover he had three daughters, two of whom were available on the marriage market.[27] In January 1539, at the same time as his approach to the Schmalkaldic League, Henry therefore entrusted Christopher Mont with a confidential mission to obtain portraits of these ladies. Mont was probably not successful, and in any case Duke John died in February, but his son and successor, William, was equally keen on the alliance, and of the same religious persuasion as his father. Altogether he was an admirable ally, not overly powerful but of reasonable weight in Imperial affairs; theologically respectable without being provocative; and above all possessed of two unmarried sisters. He was linked to the Lutherans by the marriage of a third sister to the Elector of Saxony, and he might be able to supply Henry with some much-needed mercenary soldiers.[28] Consequently when the king sent a three-man mission to Cleves early in March to sound out the possibilities of an alliance, the omens were good. By the middle of that month the news was also good. The Duke of Saxony was willing to promote a deal and the ambassadors had heard ecstatic praise of Anne, the older daughter, who (they had been told) far exceeded the Duchess of Milan in beauty and accomplishments.[29] However, Duke William was playing hard to get. He wanted a humble approach from the English, and that King Henry was unwilling to provide. So Anne was already contracted to the Duke of Lorraine, and portraits of the two girls were not available. He was also unwilling to send an embassy to England; 'The further we go,' as Edward Carne complained, 'the more delays appear in this matter.' Early in July a further envoy was sent to hasten the proceedings and Hans Holbein was dispatched to provide the portrait.[30] By the end of August he was back with the paintings, and Duke William had at last become convinced that it was in his interest to settle the matter. On 4 September he commissioned an embassy, and it arrived in England on the 24th. Anne's pre-contract was brushed aside, and it was upon her rather than upon Aemilia that the negotiations focussed. By 6 October a marriage contract had been signed and an end to Henry's two years of widowerhood was in sight.[31] Given that Jane had been unavailable to him for several months before her death, he appears to have abstained from sexual activity for about three years before his marriage to Anne. He was frequently described as 'merry' during that period, but there was no gossip about his 'amours', so perhaps his abstinence was virtual as well as real. Either way it seemed that he was getting difficult to arouse, and that did not bode well for his totally inexperienced bride. Anne had a more difficult task ahead of her than either of them realised.

Early in December she set off on her journey from Dusseldorf, royally escorted and proceeded by way of Antwerp and Gravelines to Calais, where she arrived in the 11th. Meanwhile a group of English noblemen, which included the Earl of Hertford, had been sent across to take over the duties of accompanying Anne on her journey to England, and the whole entourage was marooned in Calais by bad weather for a fortnight.[32] Whether Hertford managed to take advantage of this delay to get to know his future mistress, it is impossible to say. Language would have been a considerable obstacle because as far as we know Edward Seymour did not speak any Low German, and Anne had mastered only a few words of English by that time. In spite of this difficulty, she did succeed in making a good impression on Lady Lisle, the Lord Deputy's wife, who wrote that her sweet nature would make her an easy mistress to serve – information intended to reassure the ladies who awaited her, of whom her own daughter Anne Bassett was one.[33] It was 27 December before Anne crossed the Channel, and Henry, who had passed a lonely Christmas at Greenwich, was consumed with impatience. The Earl of Hertford had been marking time since his sister's death. He had, of course, attended her obsequies, but apart from a few small grants had obtained no marks of special favour since then. He had served on the Earl Marshall's court for the trial of Lord Montague and the Marquis of Exeter in the wake of the so-called 'Exeter conspiracy' of 1538, but that was an expected duty for a peer with his court connections, and carried no particular merit or reward.[34] He had also been busy in the king's service raising men in connection with the general mobilisation which accompanied the invasion scare of 1539. He was a soldier by training, but there is no sign as yet that the king placed any particular reliance on his military services. He had, as we have seen, relied heavily on royal favour in resolving his land dispute with Lord Lisle, but by 1538 he was involved in another quarrel of a similar nature, and on this occasion the signals of favour are a good deal more ambiguous. This involved lands in Gloucestershire which had originally been conveyed to Lord Giles Dawbeney by Sir John Bassett, Honor Lisle's first husband.[35] This conveyance had been made in tail male, and in due course was inherited by Giles's son, Henry, but Henry Dawbeney's failure to produce a son in turn left the reversionary right to Bassett's son, James. Henry had entered into a bond for 5,000 marks to respect James Bassett's rights, but the Statute of Uses gave him the opportunity to dispose of these lands without forfeiting his bond, and this he proposed to do by selling them to the Earl of Hertford. A legal battle therefore developed between Lady Lisle, who was trying to protect her son's interests, and Hertford and Dawbeney, who were anxious to complete their sale.[36]

In May 1538 Hugh Yeo informed Lady Lisle that Dawbeney's need for money was acute, and that he was pressing for the sale. At the same time the lawyers agreed that the reversionary rights of James Bassett were good, but only if Dawbeney did not sell. Then on 19 July Hertford and Dawbeney drew up an indenture which conveyed the disputed estates, together with some other lands, to Seymour in order to hold reversion and fee farm until Dawbeney's death. The Lisles were advised that their only remedy lay in a petition to the king, unless they wanted to sue upon

Dawbeney's decease, but they were warned against acting in this way against any 'great personage'. In this case the reference appears to be to Hertford, who seems to have persuaded Henry in July to create his colleague as Earl of Bridgewater.[37] There is no other explanation for this elevation apart from the circumstances of the sale, because Dawbeney appears to have lowered his price in return for other 'benefits and kindnesses shown and done unto him'. However at this point Thomas Cromwell intervened against the earls, and persuaded the king to take a hand. As a result the indenture of the 19th specified that the estate should be assured to Seymour by some due process of law not later than 6 November following. By 20 September the king's favour to the Lisles was becoming apparent and a series of letters was issued by him to stay any transaction which Hertford and Dawbeney thought that they had. On 15 November it was reported that the king had forbidden them to meddle with James Bassett's inheritance, and a few days later that he had spoken with them and so 'shaken them up' that they had promised to interfere no more.[38] Dawbeney was bound in a recognisance of £10,000 to abandon the covenants between Seymour and himself, and the Earl of Hertford released his interests in the Gloucestershire estates. So he was thwarted by the king's intervention, and that indicates that his favour was by no means secure. Nevertheless in November 1538 he was invited to a select royal banquet, and in August 1539 Henry visited him at Wolf Hall for several days. The king seems to have been irritated by Hertford's interference in the Bassett inheritance, which caused him to make some disparaging remarks about the latter's integrity, but his favour was by no means withdrawn.[39] What seems to have happened after Jane's death was that Edward Seymour could no longer rely upon the king's support no matter what the merits of his case. His favour became conditional, and in the case of his dispute with Lady Lisle proved to be no match for the influence of Thomas Cromwell. He was, for the time being at least, not a man of power. However, this helped him to survive the collapse of the Cleves marriage and the fall of Cromwell which accompanied it, and he was elected to the Order of the Garter on 9 January 1541, which was a sure sign of renewed approval.[40]

Less conspicuous but equally significant in its way was the favour bestowed on Jane's other brother, Thomas. Already a Gentleman of the Privy Chamber, he was, as we have seen, at sea with Sir John Dudley in the spring of 1537, where his service was well-received. The queen's death appears to have made no difference to his position, perhaps because he was not as close to the king as Edward. In 1539 he carried out a favourable exchange of lands with Sir Andrew Lang which was, rather unusually, confirmed by Act of Parliament, which was Cromwell's way of putting it beyond legal challenge, a step which had significantly not been taken over the Dawbeney/Seymour indentures.[41] He was undoubtedly seen as a soldier, and was one of the challengers in the jousts held in honour of Anne of Cleves. Ironically these took place on 28 May 1540, when the king was already deep in plans to divorce her, but that was not permitted to spoil the spectacle, in which Thomas apparently distinguished himself. Afterwards he feasted the members of the House of Commons, which was perhaps his way of celebrating. That he was a man accustomed to violence is indicated by the fact that on 12 September 1540 Edward Rogers was bound in a recognisance of £1,000 to keep the peace with him. The circumstances of this fracas are unknown, but the fact that the recognisance was given that way suggests that his influence with the council was the greater rather than that he was the injured party.[42] He was named to that council five days before Henry's death, and although there is some suggestion that the king vetoed that appointment, he was nevertheless nominated as an assistant to the executors of the king's will. Thanks to his brother's influence, he became Lord Seymour of Sudeley and Lord Admiral in 1547, after Henry's death. In the same year he also became a

Knight of the Garter. Although he owed his initial promotion to his relationship with Queen Jane, after her death, like his brother, he relied upon his own qualities, which commended themselves to the king – up to a point.

A more surprising, although short-lived, aspect of Jane's legacy was the foundation of two new religious houses. Given that Henry was busy dissolving monasteries at this time, these must have been due to her intervention, although they did not survive for very long. Both had succumbed before Waltham Abbey became the last house to surrender in March 1540. The first was a nunnery at Stixwold in Lincolnshire, erected on the site of the suppressed Cistercian monastery of the same name, which was granted the site, church and all the lands of the former house.[43] This was erected in June 1537, especially for the purpose of praying for the 'good estate of the king and his consort Queen Jane', and Mary Missenden was appointed as prioress. This may have been connected with Jane's pregnancy at that time, and indicates that the king was not as opposed to the idea of intercessory prayer as has been suggested. He was uncertain about the doctrine of purgatory, but appears to have had no doubts about the value of such prayer to the living. Alternatively, this has been seen as a mere optical illusion, designed to resolve a technical problem caused by the decision to remove the community from Stanfield, which had been licensed to continue.[44] The nuns relocated to Stixwold had complained that they could not afford the dues to the Crown, and the 'refoundation' was a technical device designed to reduce those payments. This may be so, but it still suggests that Henry was not indifferent to his own spiritual needs, or those of his consort, and that no general decision to dissolve all houses had been taken as early as June 1537. The second foundation was at Bisham in Berkshire and was completed in December 1537, after the queen's death, to pray for the good estate of the king and for the soul of the 'late Queen Jane'.[45] This had originated in June 1536 with a grant to the king by William Barlow, Bishop of St David's, the commendatory prior of the old house, on behalf of himself and thirteen monks, of the site and property of Bisham. Henry then decided to move the community of Chertsey, Surrey, to Bisham and to call the resulting re-foundation 'King Henry VIII's new monastery of the Holy Trinity of Bastelsham'. John Cordrey, 'monk of the said order' (of St Benedict), was to be the abbot. A charter of 6 July 1537 had conveyed some of the property of St Peter's, Chertsey to the new house, and the grant of the remaining property of Bisham was made in December. It has been argued that the sole cause of this elaborate manoeuvre was the king's desire to secure control of Chobham Park, long a coveted hunting ground in the possession of the abbey. However, the pious provisions of the foundation would seem to argue a more altruistic intention.[46] The new Stixwold surrendered in September 1539 and the new Bisham not long after, so if the king did intend a pious memorial to his wife, the intention did not long survive.

The history of these foundations appear to track the king's marriage. The original idea at Stixwold was probably a thanks offering for Henry's new bride, and the grant of the Chertsey property connected to her pregnancy. However, by the time that the process was completed, Jane was dead and the foundation became a chantry for the repose of her soul. Together these foundations cast an interesting light on Henry's piety, and on the extent to which he was prepared to be influenced by a woman for whom he held the deepest affection. Alternatively they may be seen as simply re-arrangements of property, a theory made more attractive by their short duration. On balance it seems likely that Henry's pious intentions were genuine enough at the time when he expressed them, but were overtaken by an increasing hostility to monasticism and by preoccupation with other matters as 1539 advanced.

7

THE PRINCE & HIS UNCLES

Edward never knew his mother, because he was only twelve days old when she died. At his christening, when he had received her blessing, he had been carried by the Marchioness of Exeter with his wet-nurse and the midwife in attendance. The record does not identify either of these women, although one of his nurses appears to have been Jane Russell, who was still in receipt of a pension for that service in 1552.[1] At the font a curtained-off area was reserved for the purpose of washing the prince, should that be necessary – a function which would no doubt have been performed by the nurse – but there is no record of it having been used. The ceremony had commenced at six o'clock in the evening, presumably because of the elaborate preparations which had preceded it, and the actual baptism appears to have taken place at midnight, so it is a reasonable supposition that Edward slept soundly throughout. The thunderous rejoicings would have taken place the next day. Jane's health was not giving any cause for concern at that stage, and the only anxiety was created by the prevalence of plague in the vicinity, which caused some nobles to be excluded from the court, and the remainder to have their retinues drastically reduced.[2] The strictest controls were imposed upon access to the prince for that reason, and several of those who thought that they had a right to inspect him were disappointed. For the first few weeks of his life, Edward lived at Hampton Court, cared for by the rockers and nurses who had been appointed before his birth under the supervision of Margaret, Lady Bryan, who had performed the same function for the king's two daughters, going back over twenty years. It was not until March 1538 that a full household was created for the prince, and its finances put on a regular footing. On the 22nd of that month Sir William Sydney was appointed chamberlain, Sir John Cornwallis steward, and Richard Cotton cofferer.³ At the same time, this household was detached from the court, and took up residence at Richmond as its principal location. A complete set of domestic departments was created at the same time to serve what was, in effect, a court in miniature, although Margaret Bryan continued to preside over a Privy Chamber which remained predominantly female. Six months later John Gostwick, the Treasurer of the Court of Augmentations, accounted for a number of warrants paid to Cotton amounting to some £5,000. These covered the period from the creation of the first establishment in September 1537 to December 1538, which suggests an annual expenditure of some £4,500, enough to support an entourage worthy of the heir to the throne.⁴

At the same time Henry drew up an elaborate set of regulations for his son's new household, concentrating on security and particularly upon the health of the prince. Edward, he went on, was a gift from God, and there was 'nothing in the world so noble, just and perfect' as caring for his safety. The household was placed under oath, and the members were strictly limited in their movements. A detailed check roll of every servant, including their age and status, was to be drawn up for the king's benefit. No one under the degree of a knight was to be allowed into the prince's presence except, presumably, those women normally in attendance and no one was to touch the child unless expressly ordered by the king to do so.⁵ One or more of his women was to be constantly present to make sure that these regulations were obeyed, and that physical contact was limited to a reverent kiss of the hand – provided that the prince would condescend to disclose one! As a protection against contagious diseases, these rules are perhaps more sensible than they sound. Needless to say, anyone who had been in contact with such a disease should have been denied access to the building anyway, but such risks were not always declared, and it was better to be safe than sorry. As far as his diet was concerned, a similar security was put in place. All foods for Edward's consumption (when he was old enough for solid foods), whether bread, meat, milk or butter, were to be first tested by reliable scrutineers, and anything suspect rejected. His clothing was to be thoroughly washed, dried and aired before being stored, and was to be tested on another child before the prince put it on 'so that the same way his grace may have no harm or displeasure'. These rules were to be applied at once, and an extra washing house and kitchen were built at Hampton Court to cope with the new demands.[6] Similar provision was presumably made at Richmond. Surprising as it may seem, given the general climate of rejoicing, Edward was subject to malicious threats, although these took an intangible form. Witchcraft was generally accepted at a popular level, and when dolls representing him were discovered with pins driven through their bodies, an alarm was raised. This was associated with tavern rumours that Henry and his son were both dead, and with prophecies of doom and disaster. One of Cromwell's informers produced a certain John Ryan of the Bell Inn on Tower Hill who testified that he had heard it said that Edward would be 'as great a murderer as his father' because he had killed his mother in coming into the world. When pressed, Ryan revealed that his source had been 'a great chronicler', and further examination identified this chronicler as Robert Fayery, a royal herald. Fayery was connected with the court, and may therefore be presumed to have known something of the circumstances of Edward's birth, but he would admit nothing and the enquiry petered out.[7] For

Henry, however, the line between rumour and conspiracy was a fine one, and the connection with witchcraft more alarming still. It is not surprising that he sought the blessing of God to protect his precious infant.

In spite of this concern, the king was disposed to let Margaret Bryan and her team get on with the business of raising Edward, without much direct intervention on his part. He had established the parameters within which they were to work, and confined himself thereafter to the occasional visit. In May 1538 he spent a whole day at Richmond, 'dallying with him in his arms a long space' and holding him up at a window for the benefit of the waiting crowds, but this was a rare occasion and cannot be said to have established any emotional bond between the heir and his father.[8] Edward grew up in the company of servants, and when his father proposed to visit him in January 1539, this was commented upon as being a notable event. Instead his sister Mary seems to have taken on the role of surrogate mother, visiting him as early as November 1537 and again in March, April and May 1538. She normally resided at Hampton Court, which was only a short river journey from Richmond, and her concern for him seems to have been genuine.[9] Perhaps he represented for her the child which she should have borne herself. She was twenty-two and should by the normal rules of royal marriage have been wedded for three or four years. Unfortunately the normal rules did not apply in her case because her father steadfastly refused to legitimate her, and although negotiations went on constantly, they always foundered on that rock. So Edward may well have been the child that she was never destined to have. Her New Year gifts suggest that kind of care, because in 1539 she gave him a 'coat of crimson satin embroidered' whereas the king and most of the nobility gave him pots and cups of the conventional kind. She had given some thought to what might please him. Her visits were also marked by generosity to his servants; ten shillings to his minstrels, five yards of yellow satin for his nurse, and a gilt spoon to each rocker.[10] Service in the prince's household was much sought after, and several recommendations survive for friends or relations anxious for a place. In theory the steward or the chamberlain should have been responsible for these appointments, but the evidence suggests that Thomas Cromwell maintained overall control, vetting each applicant in what would now a days be known as a security check.

As a child, Edward was reckoned to be beautiful, or at least that is what the tactful diplomats who were admitted to his presence wrote in their dispatches. All these comments were written with one eye on the King of England and cannot necessarily be taken at face value. Lord Chancellor Audley carefully expressed the opinion that he was 'so goodly a child of his age, so merry, so pleasant' and with 'a good and loving countenance' that he was quite dazzled.[11] From all this we can perhaps conclude that he was a happy and well-nourished child. The only portrait painted of him at this stage of his life, which was given by Hans Holbein to the king at New Year 1539, shows a podgy, white-skinned infant wearing adult clothes and staring solemnly out of the canvas. Beautiful by Renaissance standards, but without a trace of childish humour or temperament. Pleasant and cheerful he may have been, but that is not reflected in his likeness. Instead the picture carries a message that one day this sober infant will be king, and to emphasise the point Richard Morrison added some Latin verses, urging him to emulate his father, and to match him in glory; 'Shouldst thou surpass him, thou hast outstripped all, nor shall any surpass thee in ages to come.'[12] The burden of expectation would have been severe if Edward had been old enough to understand it. For the time being he was content to soak up the flattery and to look out for the next meal. At what stage he was weaned is not known, but it would probably have been about the time of his first birthday. The appointment of Sybil Penne as his dry-nurse in October 1538 may well have marked the time when the wet-nurses were stood down.[13]

Nor was he always co-operative and good-humoured. There was an embarrassing incident with the ambassadors of the Schmalkaldic League when they came to negotiate Henry's possible admission to that union in the early summer of 1539. Edward was duly paraded for inspection in the arms of Sybil Penne, but he took fright at the sight of the bearded strangers, and buried his face in Sybil's shoulder, resisting all her attempts to coax him out. Henry Bourchier, the Earl of Essex, did his best, and managed to get a laugh out of the child. But it was no use; as soon as the Germans approached again he 'ever cryed and turned away his face', and they were forced to withdraw 'for all the labour taken' with no more than the sight of a wailing infant.[14] Both Essex and Stephen Gardiner attributed this rejection of the Lutheran mission symbolically as indicating Edward's godliness, and the former exclaimed after they had departed that the prince clearly knew 'that I am thy father's true man and thine, and that these others be false knaves'. Henry eventually came to the same conclusion and the mission departed at the end of the summer with nothing accomplished. This encounter appears to have taken place at Havering, where Edward spent quite a lot of time in the summer of 1539, in preference to Richmond, in order to secure the benefit of the country air. His health generally was good, and he grew up rapidly. In the summer of 1538 Thomas Audley reported that he 'waxeth firm and stiff', and would probably be able to walk if his nurses would permit it. They, however were being suitably cautious and would not allow him to go unaided 'till he come above a year of age'.[15] The physicians resident in his household probably endorsed this caution, and seem generally to have fretted over him, taking his temperature and fussing over what he ate. They must have driven his actual carers mad, but the latter knew better than to complain against what were clearly the king's orders. Then quite suddenly in October 1541, just as Henry was returning from his progress to the north,

Edward went down with a quartan ague (a kind of influenza), which was most unusual ailment for a child of his age. The king was fearful and depressed, and for ten days the child's life hung in the balance. He summoned the best doctors from across the country, and one of them told the French ambassador that the child was so fat and unhealthy that he could not be expected to survive. This jaundiced view does not appear to have been typical, and in any case his prognostication proved wide of the mark. With or without medical assistance, in about a fortnight Edward had thrown off the fever and was soon agitating to be allowed to eat meat, an indulgence forbidden him during his illness.[16] William Butts, who was the doctor in attendance at that point, reluctantly conceded, and soon the patient was telling him to go away, which Butts rightly interpreted to mean that his work in the sickroom was over. In spite of the opinion of one doctor, Edward's natural resilience argues that his basic health was good, and that his precociousness was all of a piece with a robust constitution.

For the first half-dozen years of his life the prince was raised, as he later put it, 'amongst the women', a carefree existence in which his time was mainly occupied in eating, sleeping and playing with whatever toys were thought to be appropriate. Apart from a golden whistle given him by the Earl of Essex, we do not know what these may have been, but it is a fair bet that model soldiers featured prominently. In 1540 Richard Cox, who had been his almoner since 1538, was appointed his tutor, but it was about 1543 before he functioned as such, when the child began to learn Latin.[17] His earliest letters would have been taught him by one of the women, possibly Margaret Bryan herself, because he was basically literate before his courses in the classics commenced. It was also at that time that he was given a context, a group of playmates or schoolfellows being assembled for that purpose. We know who some of these were, and there were girls as well as boys. Jane Grey was one, and Jane Dormer, the granddaughter of his chamberlain Sir William Sydney another, Henry Brandon, soon (1545) to be Duke of Suffolk, and his favourite, Barnaby Fitzpatrick. Robert Dudley, the son of Sir John, may also have been a member, although he would have been ten in 1543, somewhat older than the rest. Many years later, when she was the Dowager Duchess of Feria, Jane Dormer communicated some of her memories of these years to her servant Henry Clifford. They talked a great deal, the prince 'taking a particular pleasure in her conversation'; they read together, danced, played and indulged in 'such like pastimes answerable to their spirits and innocency of years'.[18] The impression given is one of childhood sweethearts, and the passage of the years does not seem to have diminished her regard for Edward, whose natural disposition she recalled 'was of great towardness to all virtuous parts and princely qualities; a marvellous sweet child, of very mild and generous condition', which is not at all the image conveyed by the diary which he later kept for the benefit of his tutors.

Edward learned fast and in 1544 a second tutor was appointed in the person of John Cheke, the Regius Professor of Greek at Cambridge, who was called in 'as a supplement to Mr Cox', presumably to give a little variety to his academic diet. Roger Ascham, who was already Elizabeth's tutor, was also called upon to teach the prince calligraphy, and later Jean Belmain was drafted in to teach him French.[19] In December 1544, about eighteen months into his course, Cox thought Edward sufficiently advanced to begin reading Cato and Aesop in the original, the latter perhaps as a result of Cheke's tuition. He was clearly a precocious talent, and soon advanced to the study of the Vulgate text of the Bible, which he was invited to compare with Erasmus' Greek version as a means of advancing his knowledge of that language. There was nothing particularly original about this curriculum, and the texts used were similar to those upon which his siblings had been reared; Erasmus' *Colloquies*, Cicero, Pliny the Younger, Herodotus, Plutarch and Thucydides.[20] No light or loose tales were to come to his notice, and French romances were strictly forbidden. He was, however, taught to dance and to play musical instruments, as well as the simple card games which he played with his companions. Later on he was to shoot with the longbow and ride at the ring, but we do not know how soon these activities commenced. They would hardly have been suitable for a six year old. In 1544 Henry also decided that his son's household should be remodelled. Most of the women who had dominated his Privy Chamber were paid off, and gentlemen recruited in their place. From now on his life was to be male-orientated, as became a prince of the realm. It was also probably at this time that he was introduced to the essentially masculine practice of hunting and was taught to ride. A new base was set up for him at Hampton Court, and his establishment was extended to resemble a court in miniature. From now on his waking life was to be dominated by his studies, and by a developing sense of his position in the world. His tutors carried a great responsibility, because 'to be masters of princes on earth is to have the office of gods that be in heaven', and Henry was determined that Edward would be great king.[21] His education was therefore to be the best that was available. Cox, Cheke and Ascham were all to emerge later as strong protestants, but at this early stage in their tutorial careers were evangelical humanists, not very different in their religious orientation from the king himself. Their appointment has been attributed to the influence of Henry's last queen, Catherine Parr, and that may be so, but they were nevertheless engaged by the king, and satisfied his criteria of orthodoxy. There is no evidence that Edward was taught any protestant doctrine before Henry's death, although his biblical studies undoubtedly steered him in that direction.[22] How far the king was aware of this is not clear, but his concern with his son's training resulted in the production of a 'Godly Imp' who would overturn much of what formed the basis of Henry's piety.

The king's concern with the prince's future greatness was also fuelled by his knowledge that in the eyes of Catholic Europe Edward was illegitimate, and that thought lies behind the propaganda painting executed probably in the winter of 1543–4 of the family of Henry VIII. Aware of both his son's mortality and his own, he was thinking hard about the succession, and invited all three of his children to spend Christmas with him at Greenwich. What they talked about is anyone's guess, but the result was the Succession Act passed in the following spring, whereby both Mary and Elizabeth were restored to the order after Edward, and in the event of his dying childless.[23] The picture conveys a similar message. Henry sits on his throne, with Edward standing on his right, while to his left kneels the queen, not his present wife but Jane Seymour. The implication is clear. The king could expect no more children, and the hopes of his dynasty were laid upon his young son, whose mother was worthy of the highest honour for having performed the feat of bearing him. Both the father and the son stare directly at the viewer out of the canvas, and Henry's arm rests protectively around Edward's shoulder; he is very much his father's favourite.[24] This had also been reflected in the Treaty of Greenwich signed with the Scots on 1 July 1543 whereby Henry had, as he thought, secured the marriage of his heir with the newly born Queen of Scots, Mary. This had resulted from the English victory at Solway Moss in November 1542, and the subsequent death of King James V, which had enabled the English King to put pressure upon the Scottish Regent, the Earl of Arran, to agree to this future union of the Crowns. Had it worked, Edward would in due course have become King of Great Britain, anticipating Mary's son by over half a century. But it did not work; the Scottish parliament repudiated the treaty in December 1543 and Henry spent the rest of his life trying in vain to enforce it. Mary was eventually bestowed upon the Dauphin of France, and Edward died unmarried in 1553. So much for the king's dynastic plans![25]

Meanwhile the prince continued to work with his tutors. Years later it was alleged that Barnaby Fitzpatrick was Edward's 'whipping boy', who was constrained to accept the punishments which his tutor did not dare to apply to the heir to the throne. However, Cox's own reports make it clear that the prince was not spared the cane when his tutor thought that the effects would be beneficial. Cox's methods were imaginative, and while Edward was engrossed in his father's campaign in France in 1544, he made use of the imagery of siege warfare, setting his charge to capture the 'bastions of ignorance'. The prince, we are told, took up the challenge with enthusiasm, and vastly improved his ability to decline Latin nouns in consequence.[26] He was not always a biddable child however, being stubborn in his reluctance to undertake certain tasks. Cox directed himself to the conquest of this 'Captain Will', and ended by giving Edward the thrashing of his life, after which he had no more trouble in that direction. The boy had learned his lesson and submitted to the moral aspects of his training without demur. He was taught to be obedient to his father and stepmother, to avoid the company of 'wanton women' (a little prematurely) and to be grateful to those who pointed out his faults. He was, according to Cox, 'a vessel most apt to receive all goodness and learning'. John Cheke introduced him to eminent scholars of his acquaintance with the intention of improving his mind, and even brought in John Leland to regale him with stories of his constant travels around the realm, to arouse his geographical curiosity.[27] The Royal Library was well stocked with maps and globes which served the same purpose, as well as with curiosities brought back by travellers and presented to the king as novelty gifts. It is probable that by 1546 Edward had his own study, and he certainly had his own writing desk and coffer, containing an odd assortment of items including a compass, chessmen and hawks' bells. He also appears to have kept mementos of his mother, documents, a comb and (extraordinarily enough) 'small tools of sorcery', which casts an entirely new light on Jane's activities.[28] More reasonably he also retained an enamelled glass depicting Christ's passion, and sundry 'unicorns horns' garnished with silver gilt. To what extent Jane had used all these trinkets we do not know, but their retention argues a dutiful sense of filial piety in the son who had never known her.

Edward's emotional development is harder to judge, because so many of his surviving letters have the air of schoolroom exercises, most of them being written in rather formal Latin. He seems to have been genuinely fond of his tutors, particularly Richard Cox, who would have been the people he was most regularly in contact with. The menial servants who brought his meals and catered for his everyday needs would not have counted in this connection – they were part of the furniture. He was also attached to his elder half-sister Mary, although he was beginning to disapprove of her lifestyle, notably of her 'frivolous' dances and superstitious religion.[29] With his younger sister, Elizabeth, the evidence is too scanty to be sure, but there does not seem to have been much warmth between them. Toward his stepmother, Catherine, he showed a genuine affection, addressing her as his 'most dear mother' and gratefully acknowledging the many benefits which he had received from her, which would have included her frequent visits and the books which she seems to have given him from time to time. It is with his father, however, that his relationship is most interesting. A dutiful awe seems to have been his prevailing sentiment, and his letters are cautious and not at all 'boyish' in spite of his profession to that effect. He wrote to Henry while the latter was on campaign in France in 1544, wishing for peace, because that would bring him home 'that I might see you', as he said on one occasion.[30] The king hardly knew how to respond to these somewhat stilted expressions of affection; he was, he explained, too busy to write properly, but the impression is that he did not know what to say. Instead he lavished presents, particularly jewellery, upon the boy, provoking more letters of dutiful gratitude, and so the cycle continued. Even when Henry was in the country he was largely an absentee parent, and so the bond between them, although strong, was nevertheless rather correct in its nature, the bond between a loyal heir and a dominant ruler rather than that between a father and a son. With the exception of Catherine and possibly Mary, Edward seems to have grown up starved of normal human affection, which probably accounts for some of his attitudes later, when he was king and when humanity was scarcely looked for.

So how well prepared was Edward when his father's death at the end of January 1547 propelled him onto the throne? In the Latin classics and in ancient history he was well seen, and in the moral lessons which these conveyed. In French rather less so, because he had only been studying the subject for about a year, so that when he spoke to the French ambassador not long after his accession he chose to do so in Latin.[31] It was, however, in his relationship with God that he was best equipped. Following his father's example and the instructions of his mentors, he had no doubt of the special responsibility which he bore for the spiritual well-being of his people. It was up to him to make sure that the Church functioned properly and that the bible was correctly studied and interpreted. The Pope was Antichrist, and his superstitious servants were England's enemies, so when his archbishop, Thomas Cranmer, proposed to safeguard this position by moving the doctrine of the church in a protestant direction, he was a keen supporter of the change. Of course he knew that for the time being others would act in his name, but he had no time for his father's favourite piety, the mass, and let this be known at an early stage. To the reformers he became Josias, the youthful destroyer of idolatry, which suggests that he was well schooled in the formalities of the Royal Supremacy, which had mattered most to Henry, but not particularly influenced by his father's personal religion.[32] Of his mother's and his sister

Mary's conservative piety there was no trace, because although he may have respected Jane's memory, he was not influenced by her. More important to him was the evangelical example set by his stepmother Catherine, and no doubt the opinions of his tutors, however these were expressed for his benefit.

The Earl of Hertford does not appear to have been damaged at all by his sister's death. At the New Year gifts ceremony in 1538, just a few weeks later, he stood beside the king at the reception alongside Thomas Cromwell, which was a sure mark of his high standing.[33] In the same month of January he was granted the site, church, manors and advowsons of the recently dissolved abbey of Mochelsey, Somerset and all the property of the house. There were no reservations and no purchase price was named, so presumably this was a gift from the king in return for his wise counsel and good service on the Commission of the Peace for Somerset and Wiltshire to which he was named in February, in continuation of his membership over the preceding few years.[34] This success did not make him popular. His dispute with Lord Lisle was still rumbling on, and in March 1538 John Hussee reported to Lord Lisle that he had complained to Cromwell about Hertford's victimisation of one Wykes (Lisle's agent), speaking of his 'ungodly proceedings'. Cromwell promised to speak to the king on Wyke's behalf, but it is not clear that he ever did so.[35] Hertford's favour with the king was almost as great as his own. At the beginning of April one Wolfe, described as 'the Earl of Hertford's servant', fought a duel with a Master of Fence in St Martin's, London, and killed him. Wolfe took sanctuary at Westminster and it is not known for certain what became of him, but it is likely that his master's influence was sufficient to secure a royal pardon on the ground that the crime was committed in self-defence.[36] Seymour was primarily a soldier, and spent most of 1539 raising troops for the king, a service for which he was rewarded with various other grants, so that by about 1542 his annual income from land was estimated at £1,700 a year. Not all this was given to him, and in May 1538 he purchased property in Twickenham and elsewhere in Middlesex from one Thomas Yorke and began to embellish the house in the Strand which he had acquired from Bishop Rowland Lee, which was later completely rebuilt and known as Somerset House.[37] With the exception of these properties near London, his estates were mainly concentrated in Somerset and Wiltshire, and by 1545 were giving him a gross revenue from all sources of about £2,500, which made him one of the richest peers in England. Although he was on good terms with Thomas Cromwell, his favour was not dependant upon him, and he survived the minister's fall with never a suspicion of complicity. As we have seen, he received the Garter in 1541, and during the royal progress later in that year was left in charge of affairs in London, along with the Archbishop of Canterbury. Although he did not in any sense take over Cromwell's position, he was by then one of the king's most trusted councillors. The parliament of June 1540 entailed his estates upon the offspring of his second marriage, to the exclusion of his sons by his first, an ungenerous action which the king clearly permitted him to carry out and one in which the influence of his countess may be discerned. This was an action which may have been masterminded by the Lord Privy Seal at the very end of his career, because organising the business of this parliament was the last of Cromwell's legacies and reflects his willingness to keep the right side of the earl, whose influence he clearly respected.[38]

This royal confidence was well reflected in the commission given to Hertford in January 1541, when he was sent as the senior negotiator to Calais to sort out a border dispute involving the town of Ardres.[39] The French King had also named commissioners, and the earl was accompanied by that veteran diplomat Sir Edward Carne. He wrote to the council on 4 February for additional evidence in support of his case, because as he reported the common belief was that the town was part of the county of Guisnes, which was within the Pale, but he lacked documentary confirmation. This was duly dispatched in the form of a letter dating from the reign of Edward III, proving that at that time, shortly after the conquest of Calais, Ardres was definitely part of the Pale, and Hertford and Carne were able to declare satisfactory progress on 13 February. On 19 February they reported that the French had conceded and that they would turn their attention to the other business with which they had been entrusted, the investigation of religious dissent within the Pale, and the recall of the deputy, Sir John Wallop, under a cloud of suspicion.[40] They were revoked on 10 March and their final report, embracing their secondary targets as well as the border settlement, was tabled on 19 March. Although described by Marrillac as being respected rather for his 'goodness, sweetness and grace' than for his experience of affairs, with Carne's assistance Hertford performed on this occasion like the tough negotiator that he was, and the king was well pleased with his efforts. That pleasure was reflected in an extraordinary grant made to the earl in June 1541, when he was given livery of the lands of Sir William Esturmy, as the great-grandson of that John Seymour who had been the son of Matilda, 'daughter and heir of the said Sir William Esturmy'. How these lands had come into the hands of the Crown is something of a mystery, because they should have descended to his father, but he had been granted livery of Sir John's lands some four years earlier, when no mention was made of them.[41] The Esturmy inheritance somehow seems to have skipped about four generations, until Edward Seymour's lawyers dug it out, because this act of royal generosity must have been solicited. That the king was willing to make such a grant is another reflection of the extraordinary favour in which the Earl of Hertford was held at this time. Henry may well have felt that he needed his friends as the sad story of Catherine Howard's infidelities unfolded, and it was no accident that Seymour served on all the relevant commissions for the trial of Culpepper and

Dereham in December of that year. He was clearly regarded as both reliable and effective.[42]

In 1542 he served with the Duke of Norfolk in the north of England and in September was named as Warden of the Scottish Marches, a post in which he served for only a few weeks. In December he was recalled and appointed Lord Admiral, an office which is recorded in the minutes of a council meeting held on the 28th of the month. Henry, however, seems to have been uncertain how best to deploy him because on 26 January 1543 he was replaced as Admiral by John Dudley, Viscount Lisle, another soldier rising in the royal favour,[43] and reallocated to the Scottish negotiations which were then ongoing following the victory at Solway Moss. It was probably the king's intention to use him in the campaign against France to which he was committed by his treaty with the Emperor, but as it turned out, Scotland took priority that summer, and the French campaign was postponed until the following year. Then, in December 1543 the Scottish parliament repudiated the Treaty of Greenwich, which Henry had extracted from the Earl of Arran the previous July, and an angry Henry determined upon a punitive expedition. This would have to be completed before the summer's main campaign could be launched against France, because that effort could not be postponed again, and before the end of January 1544 the king had named the Duke of Suffolk to lead this glorified raid. On 2 February Suffolk accepted the command of 15,000 men for this purpose and asked that Hertford and Lisle should accompany him.[44] However, before the month was out the king had changed his mind again and recalled Suffolk to accompany him to France. The Earl of Hertford was appointed to command the Scottish expedition in his place, and this inevitably led to delays. The idea was to attack Edinburgh direct from the sea and there were difficulties in assembling enough ships for an amphibious operation on this scale. The weather was also foul, and these factors, combined with the need for Hertford to familiarise himself with his command, meant that it was 2 May before the expedition cleared the Tyne on its way to Leith.[45] Thereafter, however, the operation was conducted with an efficiency which reflects great credit upon the commanders, and particularly upon the Earl of Hertford. Leith was stormed and plundered on 3 May, and the great gate of Edinburgh blown in with a culverin on the 8th. The town was torched, and English horsemen raided as far as the gates of Stirling. The destruction was immense, and the loot considerable, so that when the English retreated on 15 May, the army was constrained to go overland because the ships were so loaded with plunder. It met with scarcely any resistance, however, and by the 18th the whole force was back at Berwick.[46] Some of the troops and most of the fleet were then redeployed to the French expedition, and the rest of the army dispersed into border garrisons to guard against Scottish reprisals. On 19 May Hertford made his formal report to the king, and the accounts were completed with exemplary speed by 6 June.[47] The earl certainly seems to have deserved his reputation as a competent soldier, and the confidence which the king reposed in him was well earned.

It is not, therefore, surprising that when the Dukes of Norfolk and Suffolk accompanied Henry to Picardy in June 1544, Hertford should be left behind as Lieutenant of the Kingdom under the nominal regency of Queen Catherine. In spite of this, he seems to have been present at the fall of Boulogne in September and to have won a crucial victory in the Boulonnais in January 1545 over a French army which was trying to re-take the town. He was not in command of the regular garrison, and seems to have been shipped in as the commander of reinforcements when he won this battle. For the most part he was in England, where he had become one of Henry's two or three most important councillors by 1545 and the leader of that powerful group in the council known as the 'evangelical faction'. The indications are that that by this time he was a convinced reformer in ecclesiastical matters, or maybe he had just grasped the direction in which Prince Edward's education was leading. Anyway, he had taken up a position which was far different from that which he had adopted while his sister was alive, and one which would probably have caused her considerable distress. Perhaps his appetite for monastic land had something to do with his change of heart, but it is more likely that he had his eye on the minority government which Henry's declining health seemed to presage.[48]

If he had not been overshadowed by Edward, Jane's younger brother Thomas might have enjoyed a career of equal success. Knighted in October 1537, he became a gentleman of the Privy Chamber and received grants of former monastic lands in Essex and Berkshire in March 1538. A challenger in the tournaments of March 1540, he was named as Marshall of the army which Henry began to assemble in the summer of 1543 for the invasion of France which turned out to be abortive, and was appointed Master of the Ordnance for life on 18 April 1544.[49] This last was a striking gesture of confidence on the king's part, and indicates that as a soldier, Thomas was not far behind his brother. In one respect, moreover, he was ahead, being involved in diplomatic missions to Francis I in 1538 and being named as resident ambassador (along with Nicholas Wotton) in the Low Countries on 30 April 1543. He was recalled from the latter mission in July to be Marshall of the army, but probably never functioned as such. He also took part in the Boulogne campaign of 1544, and was appointed Vice-Admiral under John Dudley when the navy was mustered in the spring of 1545.[50] In 1543 he was a hopeful suitor for the hand of Lady Latimer, a circumstance which may explain his coolness towards the Duke of Norfolk's approaches on behalf of his daughter Mary, but in the event was forced to give way to the king, who made the said Lady Latimer his sixth queen. Thomas remained unmarried until the king's death again made the lady available, when he wasted no time in securing his prize. Unlike his brother, he was eligible to sit in the House of Commons and was knight of the shire for Wiltshire in 1545, although what he may have accomplished during the session is not known.[51] Rather surprisingly, this seems to have been the only occasion on which he sat; perhaps before that he was too busy being a courtier. It was no doubt for his services in the Privy Chamber that he received Hampton Place in London in November 1545 and carried out numerous profitable exchanges of land with the king during these years.[52] At the end of Henry's life, in January 1547, his lands were estimated to be worth £458 a year; not in the same league as his brother, and maybe the source of that jealousy which was already beginning to fester.[53] We do not know which of her brothers Jane favoured, but it was probably the 'wise' and crafty Edward, who was closer to her in temperament than the apparently hot-headed and passionate Thomas, whose dislike of his brother was to play a leading part in the drama of the minority government which Henry left behind.

8

THE LEGACY

Jane's household was not immediately dissolved upon her death. Indeed it seems to have preserved a shadowy existence until January 1540, when most of it was absorbed into the establishment then being created for Queen Anne. On the 5th of that month a list was drawn up 'of certain of the Queen's Ordinary as yet to no place appointed', containing over 100 names, plus thirty unnamed menials, whose wages had apparently continued to be paid by the receivers of her estates.[1] The jointure for Anne of Cleves was separately created, and the bulk of Jane's lands continued in the hands of the Crown. On 12 April 1540 the manor and lordship of Langley in Buckinghamshire and Berkshire, described as a 'parcel of the lands of the late Queen Jane', was annexed to the honour of Windsor; and among the grants for March appears one to Sir Richard Longe of the Privy Chamber to be the steward of sundry manors in Kent 'in the king's hands by the death of Queen Jane'.[2] So it appears that while some of her estate may have been used to create Anne's jointure, the bulk of it was not so allocated, and this is confirmed by the grants of several leases of property, described as lately in the possession of Queen Jane. Some of the lands given to Queen Anne were continued to her after the breakdown of her marriage, as part of the king's settlement, while more were absorbed into the jointure created for Queen Catherine Howard.

It appears that Jane's lands were not so used, although whether for practical or sentimental reasons cannot be ascertained. Henry struggled with his relationships after Jane's death. Notoriously, he was unable to consummate his marriage to Anne of Cleves, and although he blamed her for that fiasco, he must have been aware that part of the malfunction was down to himself. His libido appeared to have recovered spectacularly with Catherine Howard, but she clearly found him a most unsatisfactory lover and it is by no means certain that that union was consummated either.[3] Henry kept up the sexual banter, expressing an interest in this or that young lady of the court, but it became increasingly desperate as time went on and by the time that he married Catherine Parr in 1543 he had effectively given up. Although parliament spoke respectfully of possible issue by her in the last Succession Act of 1543, everyone knew by then that this was a forlorn hope.[4] What the king was looking for in his last marriage was a comfortable companion, not a bedfellow, and although this was difficult for her, she must have known what she was taking on. We cannot of course be sure in so private a matter, but it looks as though Jane took her husband's manhood to the grave with her and it is quite likely that Edward represented the last flicker of his virility.

Edward was never created Prince of Wales, although he is often referred to as such in the diplomatic correspondence of the period. However, there was never any doubt that he was his father's heir. He lived his life surrounded by luxury, his clothes made of the finest materials and his rooms hung with Flemish tapestries of the best weave showing scenes of classical and biblical events. Even his cutlery was set with precious stones, and his most prized possession was a jewelled dagger on a rope of pearls.[5] A portrait of him, painted in 1546, leaves us in no doubt as to the hopes which were reposed in him, because he faces the viewer in an imitation of his father's classic pose, with his hands on his hips and a codpiece far too prominent for an eight-year-old. His clothes are a little too big for him and his whole posture intended to remind us of whose son he was, and whose shoes he was expected to fill.[6] As we have seen, he moved around a good deal, and the base at Richmond seems after the first few years to have been only one of his locations. In January 1540 there is a reference to 'the prince's lodgings' in the front court at Hampton Court, which were occupied by various favoured courtiers when Edward did not need them; and in December of the same year to monthly repairs to 'the prince's place at Enfield'. At other times he was at Greenwich, Ashridge, Hatfield, Hertford, and various other royal properties within easy reach of London.[7] He seems, however, not to have moved out of the charmed circle of the Home Counties, possibly because of the king's desire to keep an eye on him. His tutors, also, were in no doubt as to the nature of the task before them. Writing to Cranmer in 1546, Richard Cox said that he was

> of such towardness in learning, godliness, gentleness and all honest qualities that both you and I and all this realm ought to think him and take him for a singular gift sent of God ... a worthy imp of such a father...[8]

and one who could be guaranteed to carry on his father's work. Cox became Dean of Christchurch, Oxford in 1546 and his contact with his pupil was therefore diminished, or altered to that of a Director of Studies, but this meant that Edward wrote to him more frequently, committing to paper those thoughts which he would earlier have delivered face to face. Above all, these letters communicate a sense of duty; a duty (and perhaps fear) not to disappoint a father who had invested such high hopes in him. He would, he wrote, 'be tortured with stripes of ignominy, if, through negligence I should omit even the smallest particle of my duty'. Everything was done with one overriding purpose in view; to prepare himself for the responsibilities of kingship.[9]

These letters have to be seen in that context. They are not personal communications, but exercises in Latin composition, intended to 'trim up' his style and to please Henry should he ever demand to see them. It is extremely difficult to get behind these formal compositions to the real child, because even the anecdotes told about him have more than a suggestion of flattery about them. His precocity in his studies is well-attested, but his political judgement may well be doubted. Even the brightest nine-year-olds do not have that capacity to apply the results of their lessons to the circumstances of real life. Only once was he given the opportunity to apply his learning in a practical way, when it was decided that he should welcome the Admiral of France, Claude d'Annebaut, who was coming to ratify the Anglo–French treaty of the summer in August 1546. Edward was to welcome the admiral to Hampton Court, and the thought threw him into a paroxysm of nerves. The king must have made this decision, but it was to his stepmother that he turned for help. His French was rudimentary at that point, so did the admiral understand Latin? If he did, what was he to say to him? Above all, he did not want to let his father down. He prayed God, he told Catherine, that he would be able to live up to expectations.[10] He need not have worried, because everyone was disposed to be impressed. He rode out from the palace gate accompanied by 2,000 horsemen to the place 3 miles away where d'Annebaut was due to disembark. Once landed the admiral kissed the prince's hand, to which Edward responded with an embrace in the French fashion and delivered a short speech of welcome, which was well-received. According to Edward Hall, everyone was impressed by his 'lowly and honourable' demeanour, and marvelled at the 'wit and audacity' of one so young.[11] Edward may have struggled to speak French, but Cox was satisfied that so far they had given the prince the basic tools to learn the craft of kingship. 'I trust the prince's grace will content his father's expectations hereafter,' he wrote. He was not to know that 'hereafter' would be so short, because within six months Henry was dead and Edward had ascended the throne.

We do not know what the prince's reactions may have been to the misdemeanours of his earlier stepmother, Catherine Howard. He was only five at that time and may well have known no more than he could have gleaned from the gossip of his nurses. She, however, seems to have been fond of him, because on 17 May 1541, not long before the ill-fated progress to the north, Chapuys reported that the previous week the king and queen had been to visit the prince 'at the request of the princess (Mary) but chiefly at the instance of the queen herself'. The king, we are told, had given his son full permission to reside at the court, but a few weeks later the Privy Council were told that although they too were welcome to visit the prince they should do so not more than three at a time, and with small trains to reduce the risk of infection.[12] The plague was prevalent in the London area that summer, so this decision represents something of a concession on the king's part. Once the royal couple were back off the progress, Catherine was too busy with her own concerns to have any more time for motherly visits. In December the prince's uncle, Edward Seymour, was one of the special commission appointed for the trials of her alleged accomplices, and Catherine could hardly have been said to set a worthy example for her stepson to imitate, even if he had been old enough to have understood it. Although they had been temporarily ruined by Catherine's infidelities, the Howards had soon bounced back. The Duke of Norfolk had never been implicated, but had tactfully withdrawn to his estates during the denouement of November 1541 to February 1542; and other members of the family, convicted of misprision for aiding in her offences, had nevertheless been pardoned within the space of a few months.[13] By 1543 Norfolk was one of the leaders of the conservative faction on the council, best defined by their reluctance to allow the Royal Supremacy to move from schism into heresy. They were strong supporters of the Act of Six Articles, and ambivalent (at best) about the English Bible. Their other main leader was Stephen Gardiner, the Bishop of Winchester, and although he did not always agree with the duke, on the whole they co-operated in seeking to retain control of the council, which meant holding on to the king's confidence. Their rivals, known as the 'evangelical' faction, took their religious tone from Archbishop Cranmer, and were hostile to the Six Articles, keen on the English Bible, and ambivalent towards Lutheranism.[14] The political leaders of this group were Edward Seymour, Earl of Hertford; John Dudley, Viscount Lisle; and Sir William Paget.

At first, in 1542–3, the evangelicals were still overshadowed by their association with Thomas Cromwell, who had been their original leader, and despite the king's trouble with the Howards, he tended to favour the conservatives. Norfolk swiftly returned to the council, and his kindred were pardoned. However, between 1543 and 1545 the balance of power changed, and two developments aided this process. In the first place Henry married the evangelically minded Catherine Parr and, although he would not admit it, was influenced by her and by the circle which she assembled around her. This can be seen most clearly in the arrangements which were made for the education of Prince Edward which, as we have seen, was put in the hands of evangelical tutors, in order to prevent any backsliding on the subject of the Royal Supremacy. The second development was the death in August 1545 of his old friend the Duke of Suffolk. Suffolk had not been an energetic councillor, but he was on the conservative side and had great influence with Henry on account of their long friendship.[15] By the end of 1545 the king was coming to the conclusion that the conservatives were suspect in defence of the Supremacy, and might well do a deal with the papacy once he was dead and his excommunication expired. Added to this, Hertford and Lisle were two of his most efficient and successful soldiers and both had demonstrated their effectiveness in the Boulogne campaign of 1544. Their importance was emphasised by the death of Suffolk, who had been his senior commander right up to the time of his death. Meanwhile the battle to influence the king's mind swung back and forth. In the autumn of 1544 Stephen Gardiner was compromised by the execution of his nephew and secretary, Germaine Gardiner, for traitorous dealings with the papacy, but exonerated himself in a private interview.[16] In the summer of 1546 the reformers were equally compromised by the execution of Anne Askew for sacramentarian heresy – a condemnation which came close to involving some of the ladies of Catherine's circle – and by a mysterious assault upon the queen which was only frustrated by a seeming accident and by a timely submission on the part of Catherine herself.[17] It is hard to unravel the complexities of Henry's thinking in the last year of his life, because on the one hand he seems to have been talking of abolishing the mass and on the other hand was burning heretics with apparent enthusiasm. The web of his international diplomacy is tangled beyond belief as he strove to coerce the Scots and to set the Emperor and the King of France against each other, and serves mainly to prove that his grasp of affairs was undiminished until the last days of his life. His body may have been crumbling, but there is no hint of senility in the thrust and parry of his diplomatic exchanges.[18]

As he contemplated his own coming death, Henry realised that there were decisions to be made about the shape of the government which Edward would inherit. He was more inclined to trust Hertford, Lisle and Cranmer than he was Gardiner and Norfolk, and began by cutting Gardiner out of the draft list of executors for his will, who were intended to form the Privy Council of the minority. This he did on the grounds that the bishop was a 'masterful man' whom only he could control, and who would assume the leadership of the council in a way which the king did not want.[19] Then on 13 December, when he was already seriously ill, he struck down the Howards. The Earl of Surrey had been out of favour for some time. Through his rashness as a commander he had lost a battle with the French in the Boulonnais in January 1546 and had compounded his error by asking that his wife should be allowed to join him. He was relieved of his command in consequence and shortly found himself back in the court, whence he was summoned before the council on a charge of indiscreet disputing upon the scriptures, an offence for which Henry was particularly vigilant. He escaped with a warning, but the signs were ominous, because he had earlier been in trouble for eating meat in Lent and for being friendly with notorious sacramentarians. In the political climate of 1545–6 he had given hostages to fortune and can hardly have been in favour with his father, whose conservative credentials probably earned his reprieve.[20] However, he was not arrested in December on charges of heresy and was certainly not the victim of an evangelical conspiracy. His loose tongue and rowdy swaggering nature had led him into even more dangerous paths. He boasted of his Plantagenet blood and spoke disparagingly of the 'foul churls', such as Wolsey and Cromwell, with whom the king surrounded himself. Henry, he implied, was a parvenu and patronised other such, to the destruction of the true old nobility – such as his father and himself. His father, he declared, would be the 'meetest to rule the prince' when the king died, and he planned, it was alleged, to kill the other members of the council in order to give him a free hand.[21] Some of the accusations levelled against him were even wilder; that he planned to kill the king and seize the young prince. However, one which could be substantiated and which eventually proved fatal to him, was that he had quartered the arms of Edward the Confessor with his own and thus advanced by implication a claim to the crown itself. He was tried on charges of treason in the middle of January 1547, convicted and executed just a few days before the king's death.

These charges inevitably implicated the duke, who could hardly deny knowledge of his son's heraldic pretensions, and it may well be that Norfolk was the principal target from the beginning. He, not Surrey, was the man of power whom it was necessary to remove if the king's plans for the minority were to develop freely. He was well-hated by his fellow councillors, as he had been for years; Wolsey had hated him, so had Cromwell and so eventually did his two nieces, Anne Boleyn and Catherine Howard, whom he had so fortunately survived. No charges of heresy could be made to stick on him, but perhaps the opposite tendency, of favouring the papists, could be used instead. He too was taken to the Tower and interrogated by his enemies. Old stories were dragged up of nocturnal visits to the French ambassador, about secret ciphers and about his loyalty to the Royal Supremacy. There had been talk at Ratisbon in 1541 of a 'way to be taken between his majesty and the Bishop of Rome', and the fact that Henry had been kept in the dark about these exchanges could be made to look very sinister.[22] Enough was found to make a case which convinced the dying Henry that his old servant had indeed been guilty of treason, and that was sufficient to secure his conviction, because even if not all the members of the Earl Marshall's court were convinced, they knew better than to resist the king's wishes. Like his son, the duke was duly condemned, but unlike Surrey, he was still alive when Henry's own death led to his reprieve, as always happened by custom on the demise of the Crown. He was to remain under sentence in the Tower until Mary released him in 1553.

The king remained very much in control of the situation until the last hours of his life, and the fall of the Howards was his work, but that leaves open the question of what kind of regime he intended to follow him. In the will which was stamped on 30 December he named a body of executors and another group of assistants, both of which were dominated by the 'reforming' faction, so it is natural to suppose that he intended some kind of collective responsibility.[23]

However, he also included a clause empowering his executors to take whatever steps they deemed necessary for the safety of the realm, and this suggests that his will may well represent a work in progress rather than a final conclusion. That the Earl of Hertford and his friends were in control of the council at the time of Henry's death was not the result of successful conspiracy on their part, but of the king's own wishes. Whether he would have approved of the Protectorate is another matter.

Henry died late on the night of 28 January 1547, but his death was concealed until the 31st, to give time for all the proprieties to be put in place. Edward, for instance, was at Hatfield and needed to be in London, so early on the morning of the 29th, the Earl of Hertford went to fetch him. The prince had been expecting a summons to be created Prince of Wales, and when the true nature of the earl's mission was explained to him, we are told that he wept copiously.[24] Whether this was so or not, it would have been expected of him, but there is little sign of grief in his actions which followed. He arrived in the capital on the 31st and went straight to the Tower, which was a palace as well as a prison, and where the royal apartments had been prepared for him. The Lord Chancellor announced the demise of the Crown to parliament on the same day, and dissolved the session; meanwhile the executors of Henry's will got straight down to business. They immediately resolved to create two offices, that of Protector of the Realm and that of Governor of the King's Person, and to confer both upon the Earl of Hertford, 'upon mature consideration of the tenderness and proximity of blood between our Sovereign Lord that now is and the said Earl of Hertford, being his uncle'.[25] Jane's legacy was thus invoked, but the appointments also corresponded to the realities of power as those existed at that time. The queen dowager was passed over and the claims of Edward's other uncle, Sir Thomas Seymour, ignored, to the latter's chagrin. The next day, 1 February, the executors waited upon the king and obtained his formal consent to their proceedings, before announcing their decisions to the peers and to the rest of the council. Letters were then sent to the Emperor, the Regent of the Low Countries and the King of France, but not the Pope, announcing Henry's death and the accession of his nine-year-old son.[26] Diplomatic contacts with Rome had been severed in 1535, and this omission indicated that there was no intention to restore them. As the old king had anticipated, the Royal Supremacy was safe in the Lord Protector's hands.

Henry lay in state in the palace of Westminster until 14 February and was solemnly interred at Windsor on the 16th, where he lay beside Jane as he had decreed. Meanwhile on the 15th the council had determined upon certain new peerage creations, ostensibly in obedience to Henry's last wishes, which had been notified to them by Sir William Paget on the 6th. There is some doubt about the authenticity of Paget's testimony, and the 'book' upon which it is based is confused, but it seems likely that the king had some such intention. The Earl of Hertford became Duke of Somerset, Lord Chancellor Wriothesley Earl of Southampton, Viscount Lisle Earl of Warwick and Sir Thomas Seymour Lord Seymour of Sudeley. These creations took place on 17 February, just in time for the Coronation which was scheduled for the 19th.[27] This ceremony was shortened out of consideration for the king's 'tender years' and was remarkable mainly for a thumping reassertion of the Royal Supremacy by Archbishop Cranmer:

> Your Majesty is God's viceregent and Christ's vicar within your own dominions [and you should] see with your predecessor Josiah God truly worshipped and idolatry destroyed, the tyranny of the Bishop of Rome banished from your subjects, and images destroyed…[28]

This created an agenda which was to run through the remainder of the reign and to which the young king was to give increasingly enthusiastic endorsement. The Duke of Somerset, who was to initiate this policy, was in the meantime not satisfied with his powers as Lord Protector. As things stood, he was constrained to act only with the consent of the rest of the council, over whose composition he had no control. So he sought an augmentation of his position by Letters Patent, and obtained this on 12 March, releasing him from the need for consent and giving him the right to nominate councillors. This was achieved, however, over the opposition of Lord Chancellor Southampton. Southampton was the leading conservative remaining in post, and he was ambushed on a technicality in the use of his office, which was used as a pretext to deprive him.[29] He was replaced as Lord Keeper by Lord St John until Richard Rich was appointed on 23 October. Rich was man of dubious reputation, best known for his part in the trial of Sir Thomas More, and this was to be the summit of his career. From then on, for the next two years, the council proved amenable to the Protector's policies, endorsing both his Protestantism and his aggressive approach to the Scottish problem. He seems, perhaps in consequence, to have become increasingly arrogant and unwilling to accept well-meant advice, even from his friend Paget, and this led eventually to his downfall in October 1549.

Meanwhile Lord Thomas Seymour had become a thorn in his brother's flesh. He felt that he should have been Governor of the King's Person, and the office of Lord Admiral, which John Dudley was constrained to surrender to him on 17 February, was no consolation. He was jealous of his brother's position, and of the £5,333 salary which the Protector had awarded himself, so he set out to ingratiate himself with the boy king, which he did by means of agents among the Privy Chamber servants, giving him presents of cash and messages of affection.[30] He also renewed his suit to Catherine, the dowager queen, whom he had been pursuing at the time Lord Latimer's death and whom the king had then pre-empted, and married her at some time in April, against the wishes of both the Protector and the council. However, the king gave his tacit consent, which made it difficult for them to object. This undoubtedly enhanced his position and his wealth, and led to a furious quarrel with the Protector over the possession of certain jewels, which Catherine (and Thomas) claimed were her personal possessions, but which Somerset asserted belonged to the Crown. By the time that Catherine died in childbirth in September 1548, relations between the two brothers had sunk to a new low, and when Thomas made a pass at the Lady Elizabeth, then aged fifteen, and started speaking of marriage, the Protector resolved to act.[31] To aspire to marry with the king's sister was high treason unless official permission had been obtained and this, Thomas rightly guessed, the council would never grant. Nor could the king's permission be obtained in this instance, because as Edward grew older he began to be suspicious of his uncle's pretensions. Thomas's indiscretions did not stop at that point. Driven by jealousy, he started to plot his brother's overthrow by means of parliament, which he hoped to persuade to withdraw his patent. These moves were detected when he began to solicit support from members of the House of Lords, whom he rightly suspected had become disillusioned with Somerset's high-handed ways. They were not treasonable, but they were threatening, and when Seymour began to assemble men on his various estates with the apparent intention of creating 'tumults', in January 1549 he was arrested and sent to the Tower.[32] There his aspirations for Elizabeth's hand became known, and she was herself interrogated, with the result that the case against him became significantly strengthened. He was not tried, however, but proceeded against by Bill of Attainder which was introduced into the House of Lords on 27 February. The Lord Protector was not present and it may be (as was alleged) that this process was chosen to spare his feelings. On the other hand, it could have been felt that the case against him was political and would not stand up in a court of law. As long as Henry had been alive, his will in such matters had been decisive, but the Protector did not have that authority and it would have been unfair to place such a responsibility upon him. The Bill declaring Lord Seymour 'adjudged and attainted of high treason' was sent to Commons on the 28th, and after some pressure was passed on 4 March.[33] On 10 March the council waited upon the king to give his consent and Edward 'willed and commanded them that they should proceed as they required without further molestation' of either himself or the Lord Protector. A few days later his uncle Thomas was executed, without, it seems, any regrets on the king's part.[34]

The debate over Thomas's guilt continues. In the nineteenth century one biographer wrote, 'Seymour was undoubtedly an ambitious and turbulent man, but there is no evidence whatsoever to show that he harboured any ill intentions against the state', while in 1968 W. K. Jordan concluded that 'Sudeley undoubtedly stood guilty of numerous acts that were technically treasonable', and more recently other historians have come to the same conclusion.[35] The debate at the time, however, focussed on the responsibility of Somerset for his brother's death. The council appears to have been solidly behind him, but Hayward was probably reflecting an authentic memory when he wrote that 'many of the nobles cried out upon the Protector, calling him a bloodsucker, a murderer, a parricide and a villain'. Whether they used such colourful language or not, Somerset's image does seem to have suffered, and when the council turned against him in October 1549, no one rallied to his defence.[36] It may well have been felt that if he had taken a leaf out of Henry VIII's book and accorded his brother a personal interview after the Act of Attainder was passed, then the latter need not have suffered. Of brotherly affection between them there was little or none, but it seems that Thomas must bear the main responsibility for that. The train of circumstances which led to Somerset's downfall in the autumn of 1549, however, had little or nothing to do with his treatment of his brother. They arose partly from religious discontent, provoked by the Protector's protestant policies, and partly from disillusionment with his failure to protect agrarian society from abuses of land use on the part of the gentry. They resulted in two large-scale protest movements in the summer of that year, in Devon and East Anglia, against the latter of which he showed a marked reluctance to use force.[37] Having done his best to continue Henry VIII's policies in respect of enclosure, he had a good deal of sympathy with the protesters' position and endeavoured to proceed by way of negotiation. This was interpreted as weakness by the council, which stood firmly behind the gentry on this issue, and by the time that he was forced to act against Kett's men in Norfolk, mutual confidence had been fatally undermined. His tendency to act on his own initiative and to ignore both the council and the private advice of his friends contributed to this breakdown, and by the beginning of October a majority of the council had decided that he would have to go.[38]

The coup was bloodless, largely because Somerset lacked the resources to fight. He whisked the king away from Hampton Court to Windsor because it was more defensible, but did not have enough support to hold out. Having made the mistake of summoning the commons to his aid, which further alienated the aristocracy, he was left with just a few unarmed peasants against the forces which the 'London Lords' had assembled. He surrendered on terms and after a few months in the Tower was pardoned and restored to the council. His replacement as head of the government was John Dudley, Earl of Warwick.[39] Warwick did not take the title of Protector, partly because it was discredited and partly because he wished to distance himself from Somerset's style of rule. He called himself instead Lord President of the Council, thus restoring that body to the centre of affairs. Warwick continued Somerset's policy of religious reformation and the two men were ostensibly reconciled by the marriage of his eldest son with Somerset's daughter Anne. However, appearances were deceptive. Somerset disagreed with Warwick's pro-French policy, and the latter came to believe that the duke was conspiring to recover his former authority. Whether this was true or not, it resulted in a second strike against the former Protector. He was arrested on a variety of imaginative charges in October 1551 and brought to trial before the Marshall's court on 1 December. Rather surprisingly acquitted of treason, he was convicted of felony for the raising of men without authorisation (of which he was technically guilty) and was executed at the Tower on 22 January. The laconic record of this event in the king's journal is supposed to reflect a lack of emotional response on the young king's part.[40] However there is some evidence to suggest that he was genuinely touched by his uncle's fate, although they had never been close and as Protector he had notoriously kept the king short of money. Edward's journal was compiled for the benefit of his tutors and was a record of his role in the events of his reign rather than a personal memoir. So the bald record of Somerset's death tells us no more about the king's real feelings than the similar note of his uncle Thomas's execution three years earlier. He had been much closer to Thomas and had been fond of him in the early months after his father's death, when he had been feeling genuinely lonely and neglected, but such expressions of his feelings would have been out of place in what was intended to be formal record.

So by the end of January 1552, apart from his uncle Henry, who long outlived him, but who plays no part in this story, the king was the last survivor of Jane's immediate kindred, but he bore the imprint of his father far more than of his mother. Of Jane's docility and lack of intellectual ambition, there is scarcely a trace in her son. His journal reveals him to have been a youth with abundant curiosity and formidable powers of analysis, interested in everything which went on around him, and particularly anything which related to the practice of government.[41] There is a change of gear observable in the summer of 1550, when the entries become longer and more explicit, revealing perhaps a new stage in his political education. This was undertaken by William Thomas, the Clerk of the Privy Council, under the direction of the Earl of Warwick, and was intended to prepare the thirteen-year-old boy for that day five years hence, when he would achieve his majority. Warwick clearly had an eye on the process of transforming himself from the mentor of a minor into the trusted advisor of an adult king, and encouraged the boy to sit in on council meetings and to advance his own ideas for consideration. That these were seldom taken seriously did not detract from the value of the exercise.[42] Edward was interested in foreign affairs, particularly in relations with France, in the economy and in the workings of the council, and on all these subjects he wrote position papers, or essays, of considerable skill and maturity. The first of these, on the reform of abuses, dates from the spring of 1551 and shows a marked resemblance to the views and even the language used by Hugh Latimer in his famous Lenten sermons of 1549. It possibly also reflects what Jordan called Somerset's 'brooding and compassionate conscience', indicating that he may have been closer to the boy than is generally supposed.[43] A further essay, on the establishment of a mart or exchange in England to replace that at Antwerp, shows a remarkably sophisticated knowledge of European trading practices. This is dated 9 March 1552, when Edward was fourteen, and indicates the range and practical nature of his new educational regime. It was a long way from Cicero and Pliny, which he seems by then to have been reading for pleasure rather than instruction. By the summer of 1552 he was spending much less time with his academic tutors and his particular friend, Barnaby Fiztpatrick, had gone off to complete his education in France.[44] Other papers followed on the working of the council and then, probably in January 1553, Thomas seems to have suggested that he should address the subject of what was to happen if he should die without heirs. This may well have been thought of as purely hypothetical since he was contracted to marry Elizabeth of France when they had both reached the canonical age, but by the summer of 1553 it had acquired a quite unexpected relevance. Edward had been a robust child and had thrown off childish ailments with impressive resilience, but about Christmas 1552 he caught what was thought to be a bad cold, which proved unusually obstinate. By the end of March his health was giving cause for concern and modern medical science has diagnosed pulmonary tuberculosis, but whatever it was, it baffled contemporary doctors. Untreated, this form of TB is a cruel disease because it offers many remissions before eventually carrying off its victim. So Edward was well enough to see Hugh Willoughby and Richard Chancellor off on their voyage in search of Cathay in April, and as late as June his doctors were talking about a complete recovery.[45] However, by the end of that month he had collapsed and his death appeared not only certain but imminent. This forced the Duke of Northumberland (as the Earl of Warwick had now become) to think urgently about the succession, and he brought out, or had brought to his attention, the king's earlier schoolroom exercise on that very subject. By the terms of Henry's last Succession Act and of his will, which it authorised, the next heir should Edward die childless was Mary, whose unmarried state threatened a foreign king and whose allegiance to the old faith threatened the Reformation settlement by which the king set such great store. It was therefore necessary to exclude Mary from the succession. Edward was in complete agreement with this; not only was his sister a bastard, she was also a Catholic and would restore that abomination, the mass.[46] Unfortunately his 'device' as it was called, had not been designed for that purpose, but rather to identify a male heir, and it had taken a long view. The simple fact was that, after Edward, there was no man or boy in close proximity to the throne. The Grey line, which came next after Mary and Elizabeth in Henry's will, was represented by Frances (*née* Brandon), the daughter of Henry VIII's sister Mary, and by her three offspring, Jane, Catherine and Mary. If Henry's will was ignored, the first in line was Mary, the granddaughter of his elder sister, Margaret, but Mary was already Queen of Scots in her own right and there was no way in which Edward was going to reinstate her.[47] His plan started with any son who might be born to Frances, the Duchess of Suffolk, and proceeded by way of the male offspring of her three daughters. Since only Jane was married, and that very recently, there was little chance that Edward would live long enough to see a prince ready to succeed him. He was therefore persuaded to alter his 'device', and to insert 'the Lady Jane and' ahead of 'her heirs male', thus settling the throne on Jane Dudley (*née* Grey), who was newly married to Guildford Dudley, the son of the Duke of Northumberland. This alteration has often been attributed to the duke, on the ground that his ambition reached as far as having his son as the king by marriage, but it was almost certainly made by the king himself.[48] He knew Jane and liked her, approving particularly of her protestant faith; if a woman had to succeed, better her than any other and certainly better her than Mary. The king summoned his council and made them swear to uphold the scheme which he had now devised, which they did with varying degrees of reluctance, bearing in mind Henry's last Succession Act, which still stood unrepealed. Had Edward lived long enough, that Act would inevitably have been revoked by the next parliament, but he did not, dying on 6 July.

So Jane Dudley began her brief and inglorious reign. Neither the people nor the aristocracy of England accepted her and she was displaced by Mary in a matter of about ten days.[49] Edward had endeavoured to take a leaf out of his father's book, in bequeathing the crown by will. However he had no parliamentary authority to do so, and as a minor could not even make a valid will. So his wishes were defeated and Mary came to the throne. His death also marked the end of Jane Seymour's direct legacy, because of course he was her only child. The Seymour line continued through Jane's brother Edward, Duke of Somerset, and through his son, also Edward, who was restored to the title of Earl of Hertford in 1559. He, however, secretly married Catherine Grey, Jane Dudley's sister, at some time before Christmas 1560, and Queen Elizabeth was furious.[50] Her permission had not been sought, as it should have been for one so close to the throne. Catherine was also Elizabeth's protestant heir, and worse, her marriage had only been discovered when she became visibly pregnant. Whether the queen's own youthful brush with Jane Seymour's younger brother Thomas had any influence on this anger we do not know, but the unfortunate couple were lodged in the Tower and Elizabeth steadfastly refused to recognise their union. The earl lived until 1621 and his marriage was eventually acknowledged, long after Catherine's death in 1568, so that his grandson was able to inherit his title. The line finally petered out when Charles Seymour died without heirs in 1748. Jane, however, became only a memory. Henry's 'first true wife', and the one whom he probably loved best. He decided to be buried beside her, and that is the lasting testimony to her importance. Her son, who mattered so much to Henry, himself died young and unmarried and the achievements of his reign, which were so important for the England which Elizabeth was to fashion, were not at all in accordance with what she would have wished. Loyal to her husband, and obedient to his Supremacy, her piety was nevertheless that of an older world and she would have been deeply distressed by the changes for which her son was responsible. In a sense her heir was Elizabeth, who in spite of her Protestantism shared some of her conservative tastes. Her church was less radical than that of Edward VI and she may well have retained an infant memory of her kindly stepmother. Just as Jane was Henry's favourite wife, so Elizabeth was his favourite daughter, and the England which she created would surely have appealed to the king. Anne Boleyn's child was the survivor of her generation and although the thought may not have appealed to her very much, the 'third Boleyn girl' brought to fruition that Royal Supremacy of which Jane had been the symbol, and her son Edward the earnest protagonist.

NOTES

1 Introduction: The Family at Wolf Hall

1. Chapuys to the Emperor, 1 April 1536. *Letters and Papers ... of the Reign of Henry VIII*, X, no. 601.

2. H. St. Maur, *The Annals of the Seymour Family* (1902), p. 3, quoting *L'Histoire de Sable*, p. 254.

3. *Ibid.*, p. 4.

4. O. Morgan and J. Wakeman, *Notes on Penhow Castle* (1867).

5. A. Jacob, *Complete Peerage* (1766). On the distinctness of the arms of the two families, see J. R. Planche in the *British Archaeologcal Journal* for 1856, p. 325.

6. St. Maur, *Annals*, p. 8.

7. Sir William Dugdale, *Baronage* (1685).

8. *Notes on Penhow Castle.*

9. *Oxford Dictionary of National Biography.*

10. St. Maur, *Annals*, p. 14.

11. *Victoria County History, Wiltshire*, 16, p. 17.

12. *Calendar of the Fine Rolls*, XVI, 1430–7, pp. 16, 78.

13. *Ibid.*, p. 303. *Cal. Fine*, XVIII, p. 186.

14. *Calendar of the Patent Rolls* (1452–61), pp. 170, 347, 401, 405, 435, 536 etc.

15. St. Maur, *Annals*, p. 16.

16. *Cal. Pat.* (1476–85), pp. 537, 545.

17. *Cal. Pat.* (1485–94), p. 61. The failure to sue for livery at the proper time may account for his appearance on the pardon roll.

18. St. Maur, *Annals*, p. 17.

19. *L & P*, I, no. 20. The entry is for Sir John Seymour of Wolf Hall, Wilts and Margery his wife, daughter of Sir Henry Wentworth.

20. *Ibid.*, I, nos 218, 1462, 1546 etc.

21. His name does not appear among those challenging or answering in the early tilts of the reign. He does, however, feature among the knights answering the challenge at the Greenwich jousts of 19 and 20 May 1516. Whether he actually took part is not known. *L & P*, II, no. 1507.

22. *L & P*, I, no. 707.

23. *Ibid.*, no. 1453. Alfred Spont, *Letters and Papers Relating to the War with France, 1512–3* (1897), p. 9.

24. *Ibid.*, appendix, no. 26. On the Battle of Bromy ('the Spurs') see Charles Cruikshank, *Henry VIII and the Invasion of France* (1990), pp. 102–5. For the Duke of Suffolk's expedition in 1523, see S. J. Gunn, 'The Duke of Suffolk's march on Paris, 1523', *English Historical Review*, 101, 1986.

25. *L & P*, III, no. 702. J. G. Russell, *The Field of Cloth of Gold* (1969).

26. *Ibid.*, X, no. 1069. Chapuys to the Emperor, 6 June 1536. On his actually accompanying the king, see *Ibid.*, III, no. 906.

27. In a letter of Wolsey of 2 November 1514, Edmund Audley, the Bishop of Salisbury, ascribed Sir John's 'enmity' to his own failure to use his spiritual jurisdiction contrary to his conscience. *L & P*, I, no. 3409. The occasion for this is not known.

28. S. T. Bindoff, *The House of Commons, 1509–58* (1982).

29. See the family tree included in H. St. Maur, *Annals*.

30. David Loades, *Mary Rose* (2012), p. 87.

31. *L & P*, IV, nos 1512, 1852. B. Murphy, *Bastard Prince* (2001), p. 66.

32. For a full examination of the events of this year, see E. W. Ives, *The Life and Death of Anne Boleyn* (2004), pp. 81–92.

33. David Loades, *The Boleyns* (2011), pp. 85–6.

34. *L & P*, IV, no. 6654. 50 marks (£33 6s 8d) would have been an appropriate fee for regular attendance at that level.

35. *L & P*, IV, nos 2362, 2839. The counties of the principality did not follow the normal English practice of selecting (or 'pricking') a new sheriff each year.

36. *ODNB*. Antonia Fraser, *The Six Wives of Henry VIII* (1993). J. Foster Watson, *Vives and the Renascence Education of Women* (1912).

37. *L & P*, III, no. 3491. Bishop Fox of Winchester to Wolsey, Oct. 1523.

38. This reduction was the result of Catherine's refusal to accept her demotion to 'Dowager Princess of Wales'. It is probable that Sir Edward Seymour was sufficiently influential to get his sister out of what was clearly a sinking ship.

39. *L & P*, V, nos 1205, 1285. Sir Edward's debt is described as 'by way of prest', which he undertook to repay in two instalments. In Sir John's case a part payment of £333 is recorded, out of £2,000 due.

40. *Ibid.*, no. 646.

41. *L & P*, VI, no. 814. Edward Wyndsor to Lord Lisle, 12 July 1533. For a full examination of this dispute and its consequences, see M. L. Bush, 'The Lisle Seymour land disputes; a study in power and influence in the 1530s', *Historical Journal*, 9 (1966), pp. 255–74.

42. *Ibid.*

43. *ODNB*, Sir Edward Seymour.

44. Ives, *The Life and Death of Anne Boleyn*, pp. 291–305.

45. *ODNB*, Jane Seymour.

46. Ives, *Life and Death*, pp. 195–6.

2 Jane & Anne

1. On Lady Lisle's struggle to secure preferment for Anne, see M. St. Clare Byrne, *The Lisle Letters* (1985), pp. 261–6, and various.

2. Thomas Seymour, the younger of the two brothers, was also probably at court by this date, because he became a Gentleman of the Privy Chamber in 1537, but he would have been too peripheral to have any significance in this context.

3. Skill in the game of courtly love was much sought after among the ladies of the Privy Chamber. Flirtation followed set forms which were not supposed to include any physical contact. D. Loades, *The Tudor Court* (1986), pp. 98–9.

4. Catherine had responded to Wolsey and Campeggio's court at Blackfriars by appealing directly to the Pope. Garrett Mattingly, *Catherine of Aragon* (1963), pp. 207–10.

5. E. W. Ives, *The Life and Death of Anne Boleyn* (2004), pp. 164–5.

6. Jane's removal at this juncture is a matter of deduction. Catherine's establishment was reduced and most of her ladies were removed, but no list of her revised Privy Chamber survives.

7. Jane's name does not appear in any list until she received a New Year gift from the king as a part of Anne's establishment in January 1534.

8. *L & P*, V, no. 395.

9. On Anne's evangelical agenda, see George Bernard, *Anne Boleyn; Fatal Attractions* (2010).

10. On the division of duties within the Privy Chamber, see Loades, *The Tudor Court*, pp. 52–3.

11. Chapuys to Charles V, 10 September 1536, *L & P*, VI, no. 1112.

12. Loades, *Mary Tudor, A Life* (1989), p. 75.

13. Ives, *Life and Death*, pp. 68–71.

14. For example, Chapuys to Charles V, 27 September 1536, *L & P*, VI, no. 1164.

15. *Ibid.*, no. 995. (*Cal. Span. 1531–3*, p. 760), no. 1069.

16. *Ibid.*, VII, no. 1193.

17. *Ibid.*, nos 1257, 1279, 1297, 1554.

18. *Cal. Span. 1534–5*, pp, 292–3. Ives, *Life and Death*, p. 192.

19. *Ibid.*, pp. 193–4.

20. *Ibid.*, pp. 195–6.

21. Loades, *The Boleyns*, pp. 134–5.

22. Chapuys to the Emperor, 3 November 1536, *L & P*, VI, no. 1392.

23. *L & P.* VII, no. 1209.

24. He allowed the oath to be administered once, because it was a second refusal which constituted treason under the Act of 1534. Mattingly, *Catherine of Aragon*, pp. 279–80.

25. *Cal. Span. 1534–5*, p. 529.

26. She probably did not realise it at the time, because it was several weeks before it was first spoken of. Ives, *Life and Death*, p. 293.

27. *L & P*, VII, no. 9 (2).

28. *L & P*, VI, no. 1164.

29. J. J. Scarisbrick, *Henry VIII* (1968), p. 335.

30. David Loades, *Henry VIII* (2011), p. 264.

31. Ives, *Life and Death*, p. 297. For a full exposition of the theory of the deformed foetus, see Retha Warnicke, *The Rise and Fall of Anne Boleyn* (1989) chapter 8.

32. *Cal. Span. 1536–38*, p. 59. *L & P*, X, no. 351.

33. Ives, *Life and Death*, pp. 306–18.

34. *L & P*, X, no. 601.

35. *Ibid.*, no. 699. Chapuys to Charles V, 21 April 1536.

36. Scarisbrick, *Henry VIII*, pp. 348–9.

37. Nicholas Sander, *The Rise and Growth of the Anglican Schism*, ed. D. Lewis (1877), p. 132.

38. G. Walker, 'Rethinking the fall of Anne Boleyn', *Historical Journal*, 45 (2002), pp. 18–21.

39. *L & P*, X, no. 601.

40. It depended upon the evidence of the Marchioness of Exeter. Ives, *Life and Death*, p. 304.

41. R. W. Hoyle, 'The Origins of the Dissolution of the Monasteries', *Historical Journal*, 38 (1995), pp. 284–99.

42. TNA, SP6/1 f.8.

43. Loades, *Henry VIII*, p. 264.

44. H. A. Kelly, 'English Kings and the fear of sorcery', *Medieval Studies*, 39 (1977), pp. 206–38.

45. Ives, *Life and Death*. pp. 354–6.

46. Loades, *Henry VIII*, pp. 267–8.

47. Chapuys to Granvelle V, 18 May 1536. *L & P*, X, no. 901.

48. *Ibid*., same to same, 20 May, no. 926.

3 A Whirlwind Romance

1. *Cal. Span. 1536–8*, pp. 91–8. Chapuys had been effusively welcomed to the court by George Boleyn, and was invited by Henry to kiss Anne's hand. That would have been going too far, but they did acknowledge one another courteously on the way to the offertory.

2. Chapuys to Charles V, 19 May and 6 June 1536. *L & P*, X, nos 908, 1069.

3. *L & P*, X, nos 908, 1047.

4. *Ibid*.

5. Chapuys to Charles V, 6 June 1536. *L & P*, X, no. 1069.

6. *L & P*, X, no. 1087. Statute 28 Henry VIII, cs 45, 38. *Statutes of the Realm*, III, pp. 695, 704.

7. *L & P*, X, no. 1236 (4). Grant no. 5 was of a number of manors and other lands in Wiltshire to Viscount Beauchamp, and grant no. 6 was of the site and lands of the dissolved abbey of Holy Trinity, Eston, in the same county. See also *L & P*, XI, nos 5 and 202 (5).

8. *Ibid*., no. 139, 21 July 1536. Lord Beauchamp owed £25.

9. M. L. Bush, 'The Lisle–Seymour Land Disputes'. John Hussee to Lord Lisle, 18 November 1536, *Lisle Letters*, pp. 287–8.

10. Dr Ortiz to Commendador Molina. *L & P*, X, no. 1213.

11. Loades, *Mary Tudor*, pp. 98–9.

12. *Ibid.*, p. 99.

13. BL Cotton MS Otho C, x, f. 278. *L & P*, X, no. 1022.

14. *Mary Tudor*, p. 100.

15. For the Duke of Norfolk's mission, see *L & P*, X, no. 1136. Mary was now technically guilty of treason, and her supporters were excluded from the emergency sessions of the council which followed.

16. Princess Mary to the queen, 21 June 1536. It is probable that Mary signed her letter of submission on the 22nd. Henry did not want to proceed to extremities against her, but whether he was aware of Jane's intervention is not clear.

17. Scarisbrick, *Henry VIII*, p. 335.

18. B. Murphy, *Bastard Prince* (2001), pp. 176–7. Dr Murphy is unconvinced that he was ever destined for inclusion in the succession.

19. *L & P*, XI, no. 65. Statute 28 Henry VIII, c. 7. *Statutes of the Realm*, III, p. 655.

20. *L & P*, XI, no. 580.

21. For a consideration of this issue see R. W. Hoyle, *The Pilgrimage of Grace and the Politics of the 1530s* (2002), esp. pp. 433–5.

22. The Lincoln Articles, 9 October 1536. Hoyle, *The Pilgrimage of Grace*, pp. 455–6.

23. M. E. James, 'Obedience and Dissent in Henrician England; the Lincoln Revolt of 1536', *Past and Present*, 48 (1970), pp. 3–78.

24. *State Papers*, I, pp. 463 et seq. *L & P*, XI, nos 746, 843.

25. The Pontefract Articles. Hoyle, *The Pilgrimage of Grace*, pp. 460–2.

26. *Ibid.*, pp. 47–8. *L & P*, XI, nos 561–2.

27. George Bernard, 'The dissolution of the monasteries', *History*, 96 (2011).

28. Statute 27 Henry VIII, c. 28. *Statutes of the Realm*, III, pp. 575–8.

29. *Ibid*. Elton, *The Tudor Constitution*, p. 384.

30. *L & P*, XI, no. 475. Alesius was Alexander Alane, a Scot who studied at Wittenburg in 1532 and became a friend of Melanchthon. He was in England in 1536, but not close to the court.

31. Hoyle, *Pilgrimage of Grace*, pp. 176–208.

32. *Ibid*., pp. 450–3.

33. *Ibid*., pp. 285–7.

34. *L & P*, XI, nos 1226–8, 1241–3.

35. *L & P*, XI, no. 1319. XII, nos 16, 28, 29.

36. Hoyle, *Pilgrimage of Grace*, pp. 359–60.

37. M. H. and R. Dodds, *The Pilgrimage of Grace and the Exeter Consipracy* (1915), II, chapter 20.

38. *L & P*, XII, i, no. 779. Scarisbrick, *Henry VIII*, p. 347.

39. Loades, *Mary Tudor*, p. 108.

40. Bishop of Tarbes to Francis I, 4 July 1537, discussing the breakdown of the Anglo–Portuguese negotiations in June. *L & P*, XII, no. 212.

41. That is being married below her station. Anne had threatened at one point to marry her to a 'varlet' (that is a commoner), as a means of damaging her prospects of succession.

42. Bishop of Faenza to Messire Ambrogio, 4 December 1536. *L & P*, XI, no. 1250.

43. *Ibid*., nos 1358, 1397.

44. Deposition of Thomas Horsham, priest as to words spoken by John Grade. *L & P*, XII, no. 126.

4 Jane the Queen

1. *Letters and Papers*, XII, i, nos 336, 337. Hoyle, *Pilgrimage of Grace*, pp. 389–90.

2. *L & P*, XII, i, nos 448, 492, 775.

3. *L & P*, XII, i, nos 846, 863, 1064.

4. The trial records from the *Baga de Secretis* (TNA KB9) are conveniently summarised in *L & P*, XII, i, nos 1207, 1227. Hoyle, *Pilgrimage*, p. 406.

5. *Ibid.*, p. 407.

6. Dodds, *Pilgrimage*, II, chapter 20.

7. It was the penalty to which Anne Boleyn was sentenced, only in her case the king commuted it to beheading.

8. Hoyle, *Pilgrimage*, p. 410. For a full account of Norfolk's time in the north, see Dodds, *Pilgrimage*, II, chapter 21.

9. *L & P*, XII, no. 1225. He suggested using Lord Beauchamp as an intermediary.

10. *L & P*, XI, ii, no. 202 (33).

11. *L & P*, XII, no. 483.

12. *Ibid.*, no. 709.

13. John Hussee to Lady Lisle, April 1537. *Ibid.*, no. 1069.

14. *L & P*, XII, ii, nos 11, 22. William Lord Sandys to Lord Lisle, 1 June 1537. Duke of Norfolk to Cromwell, 3 June.

15. *Ibid.*, no. 242.

16. John Hussee to Lady Lisle, 21 July 1537. *Ibid.*, no. 298.

17. Loades, *Mary Tudor*, p. 104. Dom Luis was the second son of King Emmanuel of Portugal, and younger brother of John III. He died unmarried in 1555. Robert Ricard, 'Pour une monographie de l'enfant D. Luis de Portugal', *Charles Quint et son Temps* (1959), pp. 167–75.

18. *L & P*, XII, ii, no. 228.

19. For example, John Hussee to Lady Lisle, 17 July 1537. *L & P*, XII, ii, no. 271.

20. *Ibid.*, no. 424.

21. *Ibid.*, no. 626

22. Sir Thomas Palmer to Lord Lisle, 16 September, and John Hussee to Lady Lisle, 17 September. *L & P*, XII, ii, nos 704, 711. A yeoman usher was the lowliest rank of chamber servant.

23. *Ibid.*, no. 808. There was clearly no certainty as to when the child was due, which would have been normal. The 'experts' were nearly always wrong!

24. Robert Packenham to Sir Thomas Dingley, 3 August 1537. Norfolk to Cromwell, 6 October 1537. *Ibid.*, nos 427, 839.

25. Dr Smythe's offence included 'praying for souls in purgatory', so presumably he thought that she was dead. *Ibid.*, no. 534. Queen Jane to the Keeper of Havering Forest, 28 June 1537. *Ibid.*, no. 153.

26. Jennifer Loach, *Edward VI* (1999), p. 5.

27. BL Add. MS 6113, f. 81. *L & P*, XII, ii, no. 911.

28. *Ibid.* C. Wriothesley, *A Chronicle of England*, ed. W. D. Hamilton, I (Camden Society, 1875), pp. 66–7.

29. *L & P*, XII, ii, nos 889, 890.

30. 'The Christening of Prince Edward, the most dearest son of King Henry, the VIIIth of that name'. *Ibid.*, no. 911.

31. The only reason why Edward had been chosen for this high-profile role was his close blood relationship to the queen.

32. *L & P*, XII, ii, no. 911. This account has appended to it 'the names of all estates and gentlemen present at the christening' in a later hand. Some 124 names are listed.

33. *Ibid.*

34. *State Papers*, VIII, no. 378, p. 1. Loach, *Edward VI*, p. 7.

35. Jennifer Loach suggests that it was not puerperal fever which caused Jane's death, but the retention in her womb of parts of the placenta, which led to a catastrophic haemorrhage. Loach, *Edward VI, loc. cit.*

36. Norfolk to Cromwell, 24 October. *L & P*, XII, ii, no. 971.

37. *Ibid.*, no. 988.

38. Cromwell to Lord William Howard and Stephen Gardiner, ambassadors in France, October 1537. *Ibid.*, no. 1004.

39. 'A book of the queen's jewels', which lists beads, pomanders, tablets, girdles, borders and 'brouches', the majority with individual persons' names against them. *Ibid.*, no. 973.

40. BL Royal MS 7 f. XIV, no. 78. *Ibid.*, no. 975.

41. *Ibid.*, no. 974. The sums owed are not recorded.

42. *Ibid.*, no. 1012.

43. *Ibid.*

44. Richard Gresham to Cromwell, 8 November 1537. Loades, *The Tudor Queens of England* (2009), p. 132.

45. Loades, *Mary Tudor*, pp. 114–5.

46. Tunstall to Cromwell, 13 November 1537 (a letter mainly concerned with the affairs of the north). *L & P*, XII, ii, no. 1077.

5 Family Politics

1. *L & P*, VII, no. 291.

2. *State Papers* 3/IV (30). *L & P*, XI, no. 573.

3. SP 1/240, f. 187. Bush, 'The Lisle–Seymour Land Disputes', p. 262.

4. *ODNB*.

5. *L & P*, X, no. 33.

6. John Hussee to Lord Lisle, 21 August 1537. *Lisle Letters*, p. 374.

7. On Lisle's difficulty in raising securities, see particularly John Husee to Lord Lisle, 6 September 1536. *Lisle Letters*, pp. 281–2.

8. Leonard Smith to Lady Lisle, 22 November 1533, *Lisle Letters*, p. 96.

9. Bush, 'The Lisle–Seymour Land Disputes'.

10. Grants in June 1536. *L & P*, X, no. 1236 (5) and (6).

11. Chapuys to Charles V, 6 June 1536. *Ibid.*, no. 1069.

12. Chapuys to Granvelle, 1 July 1536. *Ibid.*, ii, no. 8.

13. Grants in October 1537. *L & P*, XII, ii, no. 1008.

14. *L & P*, XII, i, nos 806, 1139.

15. *Ibid.*, ii, nos 1199, 1207, 1227. Hoyle, *Pilgrimage of Grace*, pp. 406–8.

16. Hugh Yeo to Lady Lisle, 25 May 1537. *L & P*, XII, ii, no. 1279. This may well be the same dispute as that which erupted in 1538 over John Basset's reversionary rights.

17. G. E. C. Cockayne, *The Complete Peerage*, ed. V. Gibbs *et al.* (1910–59).

18. *L & P*, XII, ii, no. 804.

19. *L & P*, XIII, ii, no. 732. *ODNB*.

20. Pamela M. Gross, *Jane the Queen* (1999), pp. 117–9. *L & P*, XII, ii, no. 1060.

21. *ODNB*.

22. *Ibid.*

23. *Ibid. L & P*, XII, ii, no. 1008 (22).

24. *Ibid.*, i, no. 457. Loades, *Tudor Navy* (1992) pp. 117–8.

25. *L & P*, XII, i, no. 566.

26. *ODNB*.

27. He was granted Hampton Place, just outside Temple Bar, which he renamed Seymour Place, but that was not until 1545. He was also granted former monastic lands in Essex and Suffolk in 1538, which included Kewton Hall, but it is by no means certain that he lived there. John Maclean, *The Life of Sir Thomas Seymour* (1869), p. 3.

28. Maclean, *Sir Thomas Seymour*, pp. 5–8.

29. *Ibid.*, p. 7.

30. *ODNB*, Henry Howard, Earl of Surrey.

31. *L & P*, XII, i, no. 678.

32. John Hussee to Lord Lisle, 17 July 1537. *Ibid.*, ii, no. 269.

33. *Ibid.*, no. 629.

34. TNA SP10/15, no. 31. *Calendar of State Papers, Domestic, Edward VI*, ed. C. S. Knighton (1992), no. 742. *L & P*, XII, ii, no. 1060.

35. Scarisbrick, *Henry VIII*, pp. 357–8.

36. F. Madden (ed.), *The Privy Purse Expenses of the Princess Mary* (1831). BL Royal MS 17B, xxviii.

37. Loades, *Mary Tudor*, p. 111.

38. BL Additional Charter 67534.

39. Madden, *Privy Purse Expenses*.

40. Matters for the Council, 3 April 1537. *State Papers*, I, p. 545.
41. Loades, *Mary Tudor*, p. 113.
42. St. Clare Byrne, *The Lisle Letters* (1982), IV, pp. 167, 192.
43. Gross, *Jane the Queen*, pp. 61 etc.
44. Loades, *Mary Tudor*, p. 109.
45. Statute 35 Henry VIII, c. 1. *Statutes of the Realm*, III.

6 The King's Options

1. Gross, *Jane the Queen*, p. 118
2. *Ibid.*, p. 119.
3. Cromwell to Lord William Howard and Stephen Gardiner, 28 October 1537. *Letters and Papers*, XII, ii, no. 1004.
4. The king's need for more children is the unspoken assumption behind all the diplomatic correspondence relating to his marriage.
5. Scarisbrick, *Henry VIII*, p. 355.
6. *State Papers*, VIII, p. 1. *L & P*, XII, ii, no. 1285.
7. Scarisbrick, *Henry VIII*, p. 356.
8. *State Papers*, VIII, pp. 5–6. Christian II had married Isabella, the sister of Charles of Ghent in 1515. Richard Bonney, *The Dynastic States of Europe, 1494–1660* (1990), p. 244.
9. *L & P*, XIII, i, no. 123.
10. *Ibid.*, nos 380, 507. The portrait now hangs in the National Gallery.
11. *Ibid.*, no. 271. Scarisbrick, p. 357.
12. *L & P*, XIII, i, no. 1126. XIV, i, nos 299, 405.
13. *Ibid.*, ii, no. 400. A report from the reformer George Constantine.
14. *Ibid.*, XIII, i, nos 915, 917, 994.
15. S. Chamberlain, *Hans Holbein the Younger* (1913), pp. 149 *et seq.*
16. *L & P*, XIII, ii, no. 77. Scarisbrick, *Henry VIII*, p. 360.
17. He brought it forward in the Curia, but stopped short of full promulgation.

18. *L & P*, XIV, i, no. 62.

19. H. M. Colvin, *The History of the King's Works*, IV, ii (1982).

20. Scarisbrick, *Henry VIII*, p. 363.

21. *L & P*, XIV, i, nos 723, 724, 1110, 1237.

22. *Ibid.*, i, nos 907–8.

23. The Council of Mantua had actually been suspended early in 1537, but it had not been cancelled, and still existed as a potential threat.

24. *L & P*, XIV, i, nos 103, 580.

25. The delegation was headed by Francis Burckhardt, the Vice-Chancellor of Saxony. It arrived in England on 23 April. Scarisbrick, p. 367.

26. The German princes had already made their position on this point perfectly clear. R. McEntegart, *Henry VIII, the League of Schmalkalden and the English Reformation* (2002). G. W. Bernard, *The King's Reformation* (2005), pp. 533–42.

27. *L & P*, XIII, i, no. 1198. Bernard, *The King's Reformation*, p. 544.

28. Scarisbrick, p. 369.

29. *State Papers*, I, p. 605. Mont had not apparently seen the lady himself at that juncture.

30. *L & P*, XIV, i, no. 920. The leader of the additional mission was William Petre, *ibid.*, no. 1193.

31. *Ibid.*, no. 286.

32. Retha Warnicke, *The Marrying of Anne of Cleves* (2000), p. 121.

33. David Loades, *The Tudor Queens of England* (2009), p. 109.

34. *L & P*, XIII, i, no. 979. He also served on the special commission for the trial of Sir Edward Neville and the other commoners. For a full account of this 'conspiracy', see Hazel Pierce, *Margaret Pole, Countess of Salisbury, 1473–1541* (2003).

35. TNA C54/99, mm. 9–12. Bush, 'The Lisle–Seymour Land Disputes', p. 269.

36. *Ibid.*, pp. 270–1.

37. John Hussee to Lord Lisle, 18 July 1538, 'On Sunday next the Lord Dawbenry will be created Earl of Bridgewater, by means of the Earl of Hertford who shall have after his death £107 worth of lands...' *L & P*, XIII, I, no. 1407. For the actual creation, see *Ibid.*, no. 1431.

38. *L & P*, XIII, ii, no. 898

39. In the context of praising Sir Thomas Seymour. *L & P*, XIII, i, no. 1375.

40. *ODNB.*

41. Bindoff, *House of Commons, 1509–58*, sub. Thomas Seymour. Statute 31 Henry VIII, c. 24.

42. Bindoff, *House of Commons.*

43. *L & P*, XII, I, no. 411 (27), Grants in June 1537. For a critical comment on this foundation, see Bernard, *The King's Reformation*, pp. 443–5.

44. Bernard, *The King's Reformation, loc. cit.*

45. *L & P*, XII, ii, no. 1311.

46. E. Hallam Smith, 'Henry VIII's Refoundations of 1536–7 and the course of the dissolution', *Bulletin of the Institute of Historical Research*, 51 (1978), pp. 124–31.

7 The Prince & His Uncles

1. W. C. Richardson, *The Report of the Royal Commission of 1552* (1974), p. 83.

2. *L & P*, XII, ii, nos. 911, 923.

3. *Ibid.*, XIII, i, no. 579.

4. *Ibid.*, no. 1051.

5. Chris Skidmore, *Edward VI: The Lost King of England* (2007), pp. 23–4.

6. BL Cotton MS Vitellius C x, f. 65. Simon Thurley, 'Henry VIII and the building of Hampton Court: a Reconstruction of the Tudor Palace', *Architectural History* (1988), p. 31.

7. *L & P*, XIV, ii, no. 102.

8. *Ibid.*, XIII, i, nos 323, 338.

9. Skidmore, *Edward VI*, pp. 24–5.

10. *L & P*, XIV, i, no. 5.

11. *State Papers*, I, p. 586.

12. Skidmore, *Edward VI*, pp. 25–6, citing Folger MS Z d. 11.

13. *L & P*, XIII, ii, no. 1257.

14. Jennifer Loach, *Edward VI* (1999), p. 10. S. J. Gunn, 'Henry Bourchier, Earl of Essex (1472–1540)' in G. W. Bernard, *The Tudor Nobility* (1992), p. 141.

15. *L & P*, XIV, ii, no. 12.

16. *Ibid.*, Addendum I, ii, no. 1535. Skidmore, *Edward VI*, p. 57.

17. Loach, *Edward VI*, p. 11.

18. Henry Clifford, *The Life of Jane Dormer, Duchess of Feria*, ed. J. Stevenson (1887) p. 59.

19. Maria Dowling, *Humanism in the Age of Henry VIII* (1986) pp. 212–3.

20. *Ibid.*, p. 31.

21. Skidmore, *Edward VI*. p. 31.

22. Loach, *Edward VI*, pp. 13–4.

23. Statute 35 Henry VIII, c. 1. *Statutes of the Realm*, III, p. 955.

24. Skidmore, *Edward VI*, p. 29.

25. On the issue of the succession, see Loades, *The Tudors* (2010), pp. 31–57.

26. TNA SP1/195, ff. 261–2.

27. Hester Chapman, *The Last Tudor King* (1958) p. 71.

28. Quite what these 'instruments of sorcery' may have been is not known, but the thought of Jane indulging in a little witchcraft to pass the time is an intriguing one. Presumably her husband never found out!

29. *L & P*, XXI, i, no. 802. Loach, Edward VI, p. 16.

30. Skidmore, *Edward VI*, p. 35.

31. *L & P*, XXI, ii, no. 260. G. Lefevre-Pontalis (ed.), *Correspondance politique de Odet de Selve* (1888), p. 105.

32. Loach, *Edward VI*, pp. 130–4.

33. John Hussee to Lord Lisle, 3 January 1538. *L & P*, XIII, i, no. 24.

34. *L & P*, XIII, i, various.

35. *Ibid.*, no. 461. John Hussee to Lord Lisle, 9 March 1538.

36. 7 April 1538, Thomas Warley to Lady Lisle. *Ibid.*, no. 696.

37. *ODNB*.

38. Statute 32 Henry VIII, c. 74. *L & P*, XV, no. 498. G. R. Elton, *Thomas Cromwell*, p. 20.

39. *L & P*, XVI, no. 465. Instructions for the Earl of Hertford.

40. *Ibid.*, nos 512, 538, 547. Wallop's predecessor, Arthur Plantagenet, Viscount Lisle, had been arrested in the spring of 1540 on a similar charge of treason. He remained in the Tower for almost two years, dying early in 1542, when his pardon was generally anticipated.

41. Grants in June 1541. *L & P*, XVI, no. 947.

42. *Ibid.*, nos 1395, 1470.

43. John Dudley had been created Viscount Lisle in the right of his mother, on the 12 March 1542, following the death of Arthur Plantagenet, his stepfather, on 3 March. David Loades, *John Dudley, Earl of Warwick and Duke of Northumberland* (1996), p. 300.

44. C. S. Knighton and David Loades, 'Lord Admiral Lisle and the Invasion of Scotland, 1544', *The Naval Miscellany*, VII, ed. Susan Rose (2008), p. 61.

45. *Ibid.*, p. 88. BL Add. MS 32654, f. 168.

46. *Ibid.*, p. 93. BL Add. MS 32654, ff. 198–200.

47. *L & P*, XIX, i, no. 643. TNA SP49/7, no. 15.

48. Loach, *Edward VI*, pp. 37–52.

49. Bindoff, *House of Commons*, sub. Thomas Seymour.

50. *ODNB*. Loades, *The Tudor Navy*, p. 128.

51. Bindoff, *House of Commons*.

52. For example, grants in April 1549. *L & P*, XV, no. 611.

53. *ODNB*.

8 The Legacy

1. *L & P*, XV, no. 31. 'A book of certain of the Queen's Ordinary...' Starting with the council and ending with 'four footmen, seven sumptermen, seventeen grooms and two littermen'.

2. *Ibid*., nos 498 (35), 436 (14).

3. *L & P*, XVI, no. 1332. For a consideration of this point, see L. B. Smith, *A Tudor Tragedy* (1961), p. 154.

4. 'His Majesty hath now of late taken to his wife the most virtuous and gracious Lady Katherine ... by whom as yet his Majesty hath none issue, but may have full well when it shall please God.' Statute 35 Henry VIII, c. 1. *Statutes of the Realm*, III, p. 955.

5. Scudamore, *Edward VI*, p. 36, citing BL Add. MS 46348, f. 127.

6. Portrait now in the Royal Collection, by an unknown artist.

7. An approximate itinerary can be reconstructed from the *Letters and Papers*. It appears that he never went further from London than Hatfield.

8. Cox to Cranmer, 13 January 1546. *L & P*, XXI, i, no. 61. Scudamore, *Edward VI*, p. 36.

9. *State Papers*, X, p. 822. *L & P*, XXI, i, no. 8.

10. BL Lansdowne Rolls, I, pp. 22–3 Scudamore, *Edward VI*, pp. 38–9.

11. Edward Hall, *Chronicle*, p. 867. On Edward's escort see *L & P*, XXI, i, no. 1384.

12. *L & P*, XVI, no. 835, Chapuys to Charles V, 17 May 1541. *Ibid*., no. 1155, minute of 7 September.

13. Smith, *A Tudor Tragedy*, p. 200. David Loades, *Catherine Howard* (2012), p. 171.

14. For the religious element in the alignment of these parties, see Scarisbrick, *Henry VIII*, pp. 478–83.

15. S. J. Gunn, *Charles Brandon, Duke of Suffolk, 1484–1545* (1988).

16. Scarisbrick, pp. 481–2, citing Foxe, *Acts and Monuments*.

17. Foxe, *Acts and Monuments* (1583), pp. 1242–9. Loades, *Henry VIII*, p. 315.

18. For a full account of these exchanges, see Scarisbrick, *Henry VIII*, pp. 458–70.

19. Scarisbrick, pp. 488–9.

20. *ODNB*.

21. *L & P*, XXI, ii, nos 533, 546, 555.

22. *Ibid.*, no. 554.

23. *Ibid.*, no. 634.

24. Scudamore, p. 49, citing Foxe.

25. *Acts of the Privy Council*, ed. J. Dasent *et al.* (1890–1907), II, pp. 4–5.

26. David Loades, *John Dudley, Duke of Northumberland* (1996), p. 89.

27. TNA SP10/1, no. 11. *APC*, II, pp. 34–5.

28. Cranmer's *Miscellaneous Writings*, ed. J. E. Cox (Parker Society, 1844–6), p. 126.

29. A. J. Slavin, 'The fall of Lord Chancellor Wriothesley; a study in the politics of conspiracy', *Albion*, 7 (1975), pp. 265–85. *APC*, II, pp. 48–57.

30. *Cal. Pat. Edward VI*, I, p. 184. W. K. Jordan, *Edward VI: the Young King* (1968), pp. 368–71, 375–6.

31. G. W. Bernard, 'The Downfall of Sir Thomas Seymour' in Bernard (ed.), *The Tudor Nobility* (1992).

32. *Ibid.* J. Loach, *Edward VI*, pp. 55–7.

33. *Journals of the House of Commons* (1803–52), I, p. 9.

34. Edward wrote in his journal, 'Also the Lord Sudeley, Admiral of England, was condemned to death and died the March ensuing...' *The Chronicle and Political Papers of King Edward VI*, ed. W. K. Jordan (1966), pp. 10–11.

35. J. Maclean, *The Life of Sir Thomas Seymour* (1869), p. 81. Jordan, *Edward VI*, p. 379. Scudamore, p. 105.

36. Somerset's lack of support in this crisis is remarkable. He seems to have alienated the gentry by his sympathy for the commons, and the nobility by his high-handed treatment of the council. His much-promoted Scottish policy was also failing. Loades, *John Dudley*, pp. 127–9.

37. S. K. Land, *Kett's Rebellion; the Norfolk Rising of 1549* (1977). F. Rose Troup, *The Western Rebellion of 1549* (1913). J. Cornwall, *Revolt of the Peasantry* (1977).

38. W. K. Jordan, *Edward VI: the Young King*, pp. 494–8.

39. The office of Protector was abolished, and Warwick assumed his new title on 2 February 1550. Loades, *John Dudley*, p. 147.

40. '22 [January] The Duke of Somerset had his head cut off upon Tower Hill between eight and nine o'clock in the morning.' Edward VI, *Chronicle*, p. 107. However, see Scudamore, p. 224, citing John Heyward's *Life of King Edward VI*.

41. For a discussion of Edward's *Chronicle*, and what it reveals about him, see the introduction to Jordan's edition, pp. xiii–xxiv.

42. *Ibid.*, pp. xxiv–xxxi.

43. *Ibid.*, p. xxv. The paper itself is printed on pages 159–67.

44. Edward wrote several time to Barnaby, usually conveying sage advice as to how he should conduct himself. See, for example J. G. Nichols, *The Literary Remains of King Edward VI* (1857) I, pp. 69–70.

45. R. A. de Vertot, *Ambassades des Mss de Noailles* (1743), II, pp. 26–7. Jehan Scheyfve, the Imperial ambassador, was consistently sceptical about these hopeful reports. *Cal. Span.*, XI, p. 50.

46. Loades, *John Dudley*, pp. 240–1.

47. Mary had been excluded originally on the grounds that she was an alien, 'born out of the realm', but Henry's (and Edward's) aversion to the Scots undoubtedly played a part. There was no significant party in England in favour of her inclusion.

48. Jordan, *Edward VI: The Threshold of Power*, p. 516.

49. Robert Wingfield, 'Vitae Mariae Reginae', ed. D. MacCulloch, *Camden Miscellany*, 28 (1984).

50. Mortimer Levine, *The Early Elzabethan Succession Question* (1966), p. 16.

BIBLIOGRAPHY

Manuscripts
The National Archive; SP1/195, 240.
SP6/1.
SP10/1, 15.
KB9.
C54/99.

British Library; Add. 6113.
Cotton, Otho C.X.
Vitellius C.X.
Lansdowne Roll 1.
Royal 17 B.
7, F. XIV.

Printed Sources
Acts of the Privy Council, ed. J. Dasent *et al.* (1890–1907).
Byrne, M. St. Clare, *The Lisle Letters* (1983/5).
Calendar of State Papers, Domestic, Edward VI, ed. C. S. Knighton (1992).
Calendar of State Papers, Spanish, ed. Royall Tyler *et al.* (1862–1954).
Calendar of the Fine Rolls, Henry VI to Richard III (1940–61).

Calendar of the Patent Rolls, Henry VI to Richard III (1897–1911), *Edward VI* (1924–9).

Clifford, Henry, *The Life of Jane Dormer, Duchess of Feria*, ed. J. Stevenson (1887).

Cockayne, G. E. C., *The Complete Peerage*, ed. V. Gibbs *et al.* (1910–59).

Cranmer, Thomas, *Miscellaneous Writings*, ed. J. E. Cox (Parker Society, 1844–6).

Foxe, John, *The Acts and Monuments of the English Martyrs* (1583). [Variorum edition, http://www.hrionline.shef.ac.uk/foxe].

Hall, Edward, *Chronicle* (1809).

Hayward, John, *The Life and Raigne of King Edward the Sixth*, ed. B. L. Beer (1993).

Jacob. A., *The Complete Peerage* (1766).

Jordan, W. K., *The Chronicle and Political Papers of King Edward VI* (1966).

Journals of the House of Commons (1803–52).

Lefevre-Pontalis, G. (ed.), *Correspondence Politique de Odet de Selve* (1888).

Letters and Papers, Foreign and Domestic, of the Reign of Henry VIII, ed. J. S. Brewer *et al.* (1862–1932).

Madden, F. (ed.), *The Privy Purse Expenses of the Princess Mary* (1831).

Nichols, J. G. (ed.), *The Literary Remains of King Edward VI* (Roxburgh Club, 1857).

Richardson, W. C., *The Report of the Royal Commission of 1552* (1974).

Sanders, Nicholas, *The Rise and Growth of the Anglican Schism*, ed. D. Lewis (1877).

Spont, A. (ed.), *Letters and Papers relating to the War with France, 1512–1513* (Navy Records Society, 1897).

State Papers of Henry VIII (1830–52).

Statutes of the Realm, ed, A. Luders *et al.* (1810–28).

Wingfield, Robert, 'Vitae Mariae Reginae' ed. D. MacCulloch (*Camden Miscellany*, 28, 1984).

Wriothesley, C., *A Chronicle of England*, ed. W. D. Hamilton (Camden Society, 1875).

Secondary Works

Bernard, G. W., 'The Dissolution of the Monasteries', *History*, 96 (2011).

Bernard, G. W., 'The Downfall of Sir Thomas Seymour', in Bernard (ed.), *The Tudor Nobility* (1992).

Bernard, G. W., *Anne Boleyn: Fatal Attractions* (2010).

Bernard, G. W., *The King's Reformation* (2005).

Bindoff, S. T., *The House of Commons, 1509–1558* (1982).

Bush, M. L., 'The Lisle Seymour Land Disputes; a study in Power and Influence in the 1530s', *Historical Journal*, 9 (1966).

Chamberlain, S., *Hans Holbein the Younger* (1913).

Chapman, Hester, *The Last Tudor King* (1958).

Charles V et son Temps (1959).

Chrimes, S. B., *Henry VII* (1972).

Colvin, H. M., *The History of the King's Works*, Vol. IV (1982).

Cornwall, J., *Revolt of the Peasantry* (1977).

Cruikshank, Charles, *Henry VIII and the Invasion of France* (1990).

Dodds, M. H. and R., *The Pilgrimage of Grace and the Exeter Conspiracy* (2 vols, 1915).

Dowling, Maria, *Humanism in the Age of Henry VIII* (1986).

Elton, G. R., *Policy and Police* (1972).

Elton, G. R., *The Tudor Constitution* (1982).

Elton, G. R., *Thomas Cromwell*, ed. D. Loades (2008).

Foster Watson, J., *Vives and the Renascence Education of Women* (1912).

Fraser, Antonia, *The Six Wives of Henry VIII* (1993).

Gross, Pamela M., *Jane the Queen* (1999).

Gunn, S. J., 'Henry Bourchier, Earl of Essex, 1472–1540', in G. W. Bernard (ed.), *The Tudor Nobility* (1992).

Gunn, S. J., 'The Duke of Suffolk's March on Paris, 1523', *English Historical Review*, 101 (1986).

Gunn, S. J., *Charles Brandon, Duke of Suffolk, 1484–1545* (1988).

Hallam Smith, E., 'Henry VIII's refoundations of 1536–7 and the course of the dissolution', *Bulletin of the Institute of Historical Research*, 51 (1978).

Hoyle, R. W., 'The Origins of the Dissolution of the Monasteries', *Historical Journal* 38 (1995).

Hoyle, R. W., *The Pilgrimage of Grace and the Politics of the 1530s* (2002).

Ives, E. W., *The Life and Death of Anne Boleyn* (2004).

Jackson, J. E., 'Wulfhall and the Seymours', *Wiltshire Archaeological and Natural History Magazine*, 15. (1875).

James, M. E., 'Obedience and Dissent in Henrician England; the Lincoln revolt of 1536', *Past and Present*, 48 (1970).

Jordan, W. K., *Edward VI: the Young King* (1968).

Jordan, W. K., *Edward VI: the Threshold of Power* (1970).

Kelly, H. A., 'English Kings and the fear of Sorcery', *Medieval Studies*, 39 (1977).

Knighton, C. S. and D. Loades, 'Lord Admiral Lisle and the Invasion of Scotland, 1544', *Naval Miscellany*, VII, ed. S. Rose (2008).

Land, S. K., *Kett's Rebellion: the Norfolk Rising of 1549* (1977).

Levine, Mortimer, *The Early Elizabethan Succession Question* (1966).

Loach, Jennifer, *Edward VI* (1999).

Loades, David, *Henry VIII* (2011).

Loades, David, *John Dudley, Duke of Northumberland* (1996).

Loades, David, *Mary Rose* (2012).

Loades, David, *Mary Tudor: A Life* (1989).

Loades, David, *The Boleyns* (2011).

Loades, David, *The Tudor Court* (1986).

Loades, David, *The Tudor Navy* (1992).

Loades, David, *The Tudor Queens of England* (2009).

Loades, David, *The Tudors* (2010).

Maclean, J., *The Life of Sir Thomas Seymour* (1869).

Mattingly, Garrett, *Catherine of Aragon* (1942/63).

McEntegert, R., *Henry VIII, the League of Schmalkalden and the English Reformation* (2002).

Morgan, O. and J. Wakeman, *Notes on Penhow Castle* (1867).

Murphy, Beverley, *Bastard Prince: Henry VIII's Lost Son* (2001).

Norton, Elizabeth, *England's Queens: the Biography* (2011).

Norton, Elizabeth, *Jane Seymour, Henry VIII's True Love* (2009).

Oxford Dictionary of National Biography (2005).

Pierce, Hazel, *Margaret Pole, Countess of Salisbury, 1473–1541* (2003).

Rose Troup, F., *The Western Rebellion of 1549* (1913).

Rowley Williams, J. A., *Ladies of the Tudor Court* (2012).

Russell, J. G., *The Field of Cloth of Gold* (1969).

Scarisbrick, J. J., *Henry VIII* (1968).

Skidmore, C., *Edward VI: the Lost King of England* (2007).

Slavin, A. J., 'The fall of Lord Chancellor Wriothesley; a study in the politics of conspiracy', *Albion*, 7 (1975).

Smith, L. B., *A Tudor Tragedy* (1961).

St. Maur, H., *The Annals of the Seymour Family* (1902).

Thurley, Simon, 'Henry VIII and the Building of Hampton Court: a reconstruction of the Tudor palace', *Architectural History* (1988).

Victoria County History of Wiltshire.

Walker, G., 'Rethinking the fall of Anne Boleyn', *Historical Journal*, 45 (2002).

Warnicke, Retha, *The Marrying of Anne of Cleves* (2000).

Warnicke, Retha, *The Rise and Fall of Anne Boleyn* (1989).

Whiting, Robert, *The Blind Devotion of the People* (1989).

LIST OF ILLUSTRATIONS

1. Courtesy of David Loades.
2. Courtesy of Stephen Porter.
3. Courtesy of Elizabeth Norton.
4. Courtesy of Elizabeth Norton.
5. Courtesy of Elizabeth Norton.
6. Courtesy of Elizabeth Norton.
7. Courtesy of Jonathan Reeve JR620p976.
8. Courtesy of Elizabeth Norton.
9. Courtesy of Jonathan Reeve JR997b66fp40M 15001550.
10. Courtesy of Stephen Porter.
11. Courtesy of Ripon Cathedral.
12. Courtesy of Jonathan Reeve JRpc219 15001550.
13. Courtesy of Amberley Archive.
14. Courtesy of Jonathan Reeve JR2600b120fp158 15001550.
15. Courtesy of Elizabeth Norton.
16. Courtesy of Stephen Porter.
17. Courtesy of Stephen Porter.
18. Courtesy of Stephen Porter.
19. Courtesy of Jonathan Reeve JR1882b46fp180c 15001550.
20. Courtesy of Stephen Porter.
21. Courtesy of Amy Licence.
22. Courtesy of Jonathan Reeve JR1189b67plixB 16001650.
23. Courtesy of Elizabeth Norton.
24. Courtesy of Jonathan Reeve JR1149pc 15001550.
25. Courtesy of Jonathan Reeve JR945b20p788 15001550.
26. Courtesy of Stephen Porter.
27. Courtesy of Jonathan Reeve JRCD3b20p913 15001550.
28. Courtesy of Jonathan Reeve JRCD2b20p929 15001550.
29. Courtesy of Jonathan Reeve JR1092b20fp896 15001550.
30. Courtesy of Jonathan Reeve JR896b7p161TL 15001550.
31. Courtesy of Jonathan Reeve JR896b7p161TR 15001550.
32. Courtesy of Jonathan Reeve JR997b66fp40R 15001550.
33. Courtesy of Elizabeth Norton.
34. Courtesy of Jonathan Reeve JR1001b66fp100 15001550.
35. Courtesy of Jonathan Reeve JR997b66fp40L 15001550.
36. Courtesy of Jonathan Reeve JR949b2p110 15001550.
37. Courtesy of Stephen Porter.
38. Courtesy of Stephen Porter.
39. Courtesy of Stephen Porter.
40. Courtesy of Stephen Porter.

INDEX

Tudor History from Amberley Publishing

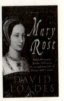

More Tudor History from Amberley Publishing